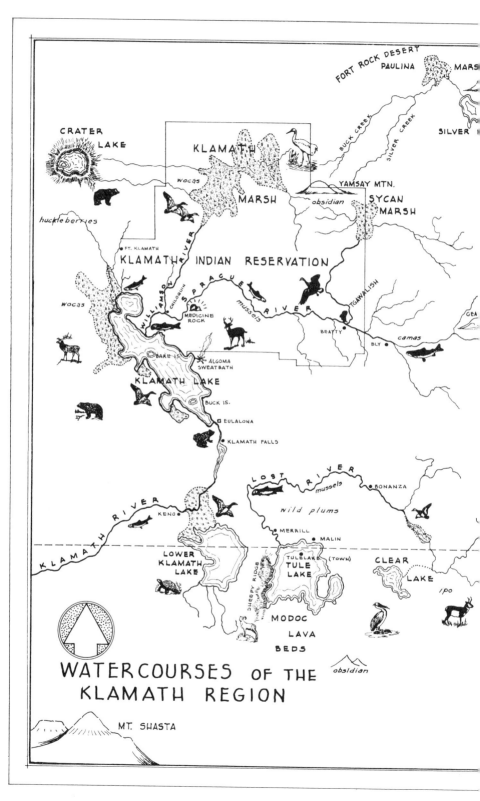

WATERCOURSES OF THE KLAMATH REGION

Ancient Tribes
of the
Klamath Country

Ancient Tribes
of the
Klamath Country

By Carrol B. Howe

Binfords & Mort, *Publishers*

Portland   •   Oregon   •   97242

Ancient Tribes of the Klamath Country

LIBRARY OF CONGRESS CATALOG CARD NUMBER: 68-28922

ISBN 0-8323-0131-0
Printed in the United States of America
First Edition
Second Printing 1969
Third Printing 1972

Dedication

To the generations of wonderful Indian women who for thousands of years kept alive the skills, the arts, and the heartbeat of a race.

Contents

Introduction

The fishing pole in my hand was still unjointed, the mud was up to my ankles, and I was still fifty yards from the water. My wife and I had driven over a rocky, remote road for thirty miles in order to reach this most unpromising fishing place. The scene was Clear Lake in Modoc County, California; the year 1933. The place smelled of mud and decaying mussels. The sparse sagebrush did not even provide a shady place to eat lunch. On the map it had looked like a great place for an outing, and the name Clear Lake had sounded promising.

Destiny causes people to make strange blunders. Sometimes the blunders end in misfortune, but occasionally a mistake has a happy ending. This one did. At the time, however, my position in the mud was neither happy nor funny, even though it would have seemed ludicrous to any old-timer who knew the country. A friend later described Clear Lake as "the only body of water that dust would blow from on a windy day."

Located on the western edge of the Great Basin, it had never been a place for game fish. Further, in 1933, the water level was so dangerously low that the federal wildlife officials were concerned about the survival of the nesting pelicans. The light winter snowfall and arid spring weather had caused the shoreline to recede over one-fourth of a mile from the islands, where the newly hatched birds sat helplessly in the sun. No one was aware that soon the parent birds would solve their own problem and lead their awkward progeny down to the edge of the receding waters.

As I stood grimly staring at the miles of muddy water, I did not know that this ill-fated fishing trip would result in a new and fascinating chapter in my life. With head lowered, I started back toward the model A Ford coupe where my wife waited—her steel telescope fishing rod still in the trunk of the car. As I trudged along, I noticed some rocks which the winds and waves had left exposed . . . . The return trip to my car was to take a long time, for here among the rocks were particles of obsidian and a broken fragment of an Indian arrowhead. I spent about an hour looking along the barren shores. The result was four or five broken or chipped fragments, a broken pestle, and one perfect arrowhead. This arrowhead is small and simple, yet one that holds a particular place in my memory, for this bit of chipped stone so captured my imagination that during the weeks following, I looked at it frequently.

Thoughts of other glistening arrowheads so intrigued me that I could not resist returning over the torturous road for another look at the desolate and lonely shores of this northern California lake. I did not know then that beneath my feet the earth contained the story of a people more ancient than the pyramids of Egypt, and more remarkable in their industries than the feathered Indians of the Great Plains or the warlike Apaches of the Southwest. I soon found out, however, that here was a profound story—undiscovered, untold—and that I must try to find it and tell it.

The search for that story has been a hobby rather than a profession. It took me to the Oregon desert in the Fort Rock Valley and into Warner Valley where, scientists later discovered, postglacial man had lived. It took me to the shores of the Willamette, Columbia, and Calapooia rivers, where I could make comparisons of Indian ways of life. The same inquisitive drive that caused me to return to Clear Lake has since sent me thousands of miles into the Sierra Madre Mountains of Old Mexico and among the ruins of the Mimbres people in New Mexico. I have examined the stone houses of the cliff dwellers and the clay dwellings of the long-extinct Hohokams of Arizona; and I have visited many museums in search of clues to more information about my beloved ancient ones of Oregon and California. In my effort to piece together the story of the successive Indian cultures which developed in this highland of lakes and deserts, I have also found valuable information in many private collections. Results of this research indicate that these cultures—while decidedly different from the typical buffalo Indians to the east and the acorn-eaters to the south—are no less interesting.

To round out the story, I have interviewed many Indian friends and others who are acquainted with the Klamath country. And, to be sure that my findings had a solid basis in science, it has been necessary to consult and interpret the work of professional archeologists.

For the scientific information on which this work is based, the writer is indebted principally to two pioneer workers. In the field of archeology, the research reports and teaching of Dr. L. S. Cressman, former head of the Anthropology Department at the University of Oregon, have been of tremendous value. The writings and notes of Albert S. Gatschet, who spent much time with the Klamaths and Modocs in the 1880s, have also proved to be an invaluable source of information.

The works of Leslie Spier, S. A. Barrett, and Verne F. Ray have proved especially helpful. Many others have aided in interpreting the materials in order to give meaning to the otherwise lifeless stone and bone objects. Included among these are: Dave Cole, head of the Oregon Archeology Department for the Oregon Museum of Natural History at the University of Oregon; Erin Forrest, Pit River Indian; Wren Frain, Shasta Indian; Selden Kirk, Klamath Indian; Hal Ogle, Alfred Collier, and Devere Helfrich of Klamath Falls, Oregon; and John McKay of Dorris, California.

I am indebted to Van Landrum for map work and photography; to the *Klamath Herald-News* for some photographs; and to Bill Burk, curator of the Klamath County Museum, for many types of assistance. To my wife, Marjorie, I am grateful for the typing of the manuscript, as well as for companionship on the numerous long, desert treks while we both searched for artifacts. I also extend thanks to my many fellow collectors who permitted me to inspect and photograph their finds, some of whom will see pictures from their collections in this book.

Carrol B.Howe

Early man moved into the caves provided by nature in the faulted rimrocks of the great basin. An eagle's nest has been built above these three caves.

1. LAND OF LAKES AND DESERTS

Homeland for Ancient Man

Nature took a long time to prepare the Klamath country for mankind. The exact date that the first Americans, the Indians, arrived has not yet been determined. It was at least four thousand years before the pharaohs of Egypt began ordering the building of the great pyramids; so long ago that the land forms were still undergoing dynamic changes. Volcanoes were occasionally blowing huge clouds of ash and pumice into the skies, and shiny flows of black silica were forming the stone called obsidian. This in turn would be shaped into the tools and weapons of hunters and warriors. (Fig. 1)

The climate also was to undergo slow but drastic changes during the long weather cycles, and the plants and animals would vary with the changing cycles. Though modern man has devoted his efforts toward adjusting his environment to suit his own needs, primitive man worked to adapt his way of life to his surroundings and the ever-shifting cycles.

Unique Culture Developed

The Indians of Modoc and Siskiyou counties in California and Klamath and Lake counties in Oregon did not intentionally go about the business of building a culture different from any

1

other. Their unique culture developed unknowingly and gradually over the centuries as they accommodated their way of life to their upland basins, in an effort to survive. Geology, altitude, and climate all played a part in the drama of development which took place. Here the forces of nature slowly made an indelible imprint on the Indian, his tools, his unwritten laws, and his religion. Probably the greatest natural force that shaped his way of life was exerted by the Cascade Range.

The Cascades Rise

The long Cascade mountain chain forms a midrib through Northern California, Oregon, and Washington, and a part of British Columbia. The range originated in a weak seam along the north and south axis. This flaw in the earth's crust allowed the molten magmas from the interior to break through and push the mountain chain up through the waters of the salty inland sea which once covered the region. Eons were required for the mountain formation to reach its present height; the process was so slow that some mountains were nearly worn away before others were formed. This mountain-building activity was so recent that pumice from their volcanoes covered the tools and utensils used by early man. We know, for example, that man was a witness to the great eruption of Mount Mazama. He may not have seen but he certainly heard the earth-shaking collapse of that mighty 14,000-foot peak, which forms the deep caldera now embraced in Crater Lake National Park. Fig. 2 shows the great depth of pumice on one side of the fallen mountain.

While the volcanoes of the Cascades were belching clouds of ash and pumice into the skies, westerly winds were carrying and scattering it over the wide, shallow pliocene lakes to the east. The resulting terrain made an ideal place for the growth of tiny plants called diatoms. These single-celled plants have their own chlorophyll but require silica to build their glassy skeletons. With plenty of sunlight, ample silica, and warm, shallow waters, the organisms grew in those lake beds in such numbers that great de-

Fig. 1. This delicately fashioned point of obsidian—sometimes called volcanic glass—is from the Gene Favell collection.

Fig. 2. Indians were here to observe the great eruption which laid down this layer of pumice. Annie Creek has cut through to reveal the depth.

posits of diatomaceous earth were formed. These white banks—
called chalk by local residents—have a thickness of more than
seven hundred feet in some places. Occasionally a highway cut
or an irrigation canal uncovers a new deposit.
Except for the silica-diatom remains, fossil forms are not
abundant here. It is known, though, that a pig-like mammal
called a peccary lived here during the pliocene period. At
Merrill, Oregon, near the California line, a crew of the Klamath
County irrigation district came upon a strange group of fossil
bones while digging out a muskrat burrow. When the county
museum sent specimens to Dr. Arnold Shotwell at the University
of Oregon for identification, they were found to be the fossil
remains of an enormous camel about twice the size of the present-
day Arabian camel. (Fig. 3)

There is no evidence whatever that man existed in America
at the same time the giant camel was grazing on the shores of the
pliocene lake. The chalky material did, however, provide him
with a base for white paint with which he decorated himself
some two million years later.

The Cascade Range created two distinct climates in the
Northwest: a wet climate on the west side, a dry climate on the
east. The elevation of the mountains causes the moisture-laden
winds from the Pacific to deflect upward and thus lower their
temperature. This thermal barrier brings about condensation and
resultant rain and snowfall over the full length of the range; and
the moisture loss causes a sunny, dry area called a rain shadow
on the area east of the mountains.

The Columbia Lava Flow

In addition to the Cascades, another geological event helped
shape the homeland of the ancient Indians. This was called the
Columbia River lava flow. Though the actual flow was unrelated
to the Columbia River, its waters have since cut through the
lava, exposing the layered structure which covers much of the
land east of the Cascade Mountains.

Issuing from fissures in the earth's crust, the super-heated, liquid lava spread out to form a great black sea of stone. Only the highest mountains escaped being covered by the creeping lava. Layer upon layer was built up to form a structure which drillings reveal as several thousand feet deep in some places.

The major result of this lava blanket on the land surfaces occurred when the strong tensions in the earth's crust caused it to crack. Long, vertical cliffs or "faults" were shaped where the rocks were uplifted. Between these cliffs, the land surface dropped, forming basins. One of the best examples of this dual action is Abert Rim and Lake Basin, north of Lakeview, Oregon. A relief map reveals that the range and basin formations extend in a great series as far east as mid-Utah.

In some places the faults allowed the waters to filter down into the still uncooled lava, causing hot springs which continue to issue from underground pools.

Ice-Age Lakes

The Ice Age was a third geological event that helped mold man's early home. During this period a cap of ice formed over much of North America, though it did not cover the Cascades or the lava plateau to the east. It did, however, change the climate to such an extent that glaciers appeared on the high peaks, and the basins between the faults filled to great depths from the later melting waters.

We know that man lived here at the time of these deep inland lakes. His caves, camps and debris are found high above any present water level; they are found where the waves of Ice Age lakes cut beaches on the mountain sides. A signboard marking the entrance to a cave dwelling is shown in Fig. 4.

Waters receded from the lakes during the climatic changes at the end of the Ice Age. Warmer temperatures brought both reduced rainfall and increased evaporation. Plants and animals abounded on the newly exposed valley floors, and man developed new tools to process his new resources. Some groups moved

Fig. 3. A plaster cast for the bones of a two-million-year-old camel is prepared by the author.

Fig. 4. The mountain goat sign above one of the caves might represent either an animal guardian or a good meal.

from wave-cut caves and built houses on the shores of lakes and streams for use during the winter season. Hunting and gathering food often forced them to leave their houses during other seasons. The land occupied by these Indians is a region of contrasts, and this is as true today as it was in ancient times. A minimum altitude of over four thousand feet causes cool nights and sunny days. During certain seasons it is a land of abundance; during others, a land of hunger. In a year of good rainfall a valley may contain a lake filled with waterfowl and plants. Another year, the same basin may appear like a dust-blown desert.

Certain of the basins which lie adjacent to the Cascade Range are fed from the springs and streams which flow from the snow-rich Cascade Mountain peaks. These are always filled, and they were once the places where Indians could survive in the greatest numbers, developing more permanent forms of villages with a more varied culture. It was in these more hospitable surroundings that the Indians added to the knowledge brought by their ancestors from Asia. Despite their common heritage, a different way of life is apparent from valley to valley and even in villages that were side by side.

Six Stone-Age Homelands

In the following chapters, six Indian homelands are described. Three of these are located mainly in what is now California: Tule Lake, Lower Klamath Lake, and the Lost River-Clear Lake region. These areas were all occupied by the Modocs prior to the coming of the white man, and each seems to have had a somewhat different material culture as indicated by artifacts the inhabitants left. Whether a part of this material was deposited by a people prior to the Modocs, or whether the Modocs developed all of it over the centuries, is still not positively determined.

The three Indian homelands in Oregon included the Upper Klamath-Klamath Marsh area, the Fort Rock-Silver Lake area, and Warner Valley, which extends north from Fort Bidwell in

California. The latter two areas were occupied by the nothern Paiutes at the time of contact with the white man and have an overlay of Paiute artifacts. Eroding from beneath this overlay is evidence of the "ancient ones." There is still much to be learned about the stone objects left within the boundaries of these areas. The soils of the old camps occasionally give up a new clue, but some of the answers may never be found.

Mysteries from the Past

From the studies of scientists and the collections of amateurs, however, a great deal has been learned about these early residents as well as about their artifacts. For example, it has been determined that they brought dogs with them from the Old World; also their atlatls or "spear throwers." Only later did they possess the bow and arrow. The excavations of archeologists indicate that the women had already developed fine skills in basketry by the time they occupied their post-glacial caves. An unusual example from such a cave is the "handbag" found in Lake County, as shown in Fig. 5.

Many of the artifacts pictured and described in later chapters are quite common, but the uses to which they were put is sometimes indefinite. An obsidian blade might have been used to scale a fish, butcher a mountain sheep, pierce an enemy, or scrape a bow. The shape of a blade does not always reveal the diversity of its uses. Even though some artifacts seem designed for a special purpose, it is not always possible to determine the intent of the maker. A blade with notches for attachment to a spear could also be fastened to a knife handle. The items pictured have been named according to their most probable and common use.

There are some stone-age objects that virtually defy explanation. The two stones in Fig. 6 are of this type. The upper stone would resemble one type of Columbia River net weight, except that it has deep grooves extending down both sides. Paul

Fig. 5. This fine tule bag may have been suspended from the neck of a stone-age maiden.

Fig. 6. Unusual stones from Summer Lake and Lost River.

Matthews, who found this artifact on a dry ridge near Summer Lake, has dubbed it a "mother-in-law killer." Lacking a more suitable explanation, no argument is offered.

The lower stone in Fig. 6, found by Mrs. Roy Whitlatch on the banks of Lost River, is so unusual that it seems to have no logical explanation. It could be a net-making tool but the final answer must be left to some future interpretation. There are times when the writer would be tempted to trade his scientific training for the "spirit power" of the old Indian conjurers, in order to solve the mystery that still surrounds certain artifacts. The two stones in Fig. 7 are among the mysteries. These were found in northern California, one on the bed of Lower Klamath Lake, the other on Tule Lake bed. The stone on the right was discovered by Lawrence Gray and is on loan to the Klamath County Museum. A midwestern stone with this general shape has been labeled a "squaw club." Some say it was attached to a rawhide thong and used as a weapon by the plains Indian women to finish off the wounded on the battlefield. The weight of either of the stones pictured would be so great that a lady physically capable of wielding such a stone would need no weapon. She could perform the gruesome job with her bare hands.

Mystery of the Skulls

A different type of mystery is shown in Fig. 8. Obviously the bones are fragments of human skulls which have been drilled out to form neck pendants. They were washed from the banks of Lost River near Olene and were found by Jim DeVore in the vicinity of a human skeleton. These are not unique. A human-skull pendant was given to the Klamath County Museum by Burt Thomas and is now on display there. The mystery in this case is not "What is it?" but "Why is it?" Are these fragments part of a skull of a favorite wife? Could they be trophies collected from enemies in battle? Could the original owner of the head have been partially consumed by the wearer of the ornaments in order to increase his wisdom, spirit power, or courage?

Perhaps they provided the magic necessary to carry on the business of being a stone-age doctor. The secret of the skulls may some day be revealed—or it may remain to challenge man's imagination.

In later chapters an effort has been made to interpret the items presented, in some cases at the risk of being in error; but guessing has not been substituted for evidence. Further research by archeologists may provide the answers to many of the unsolved questions. Until that time, however, we can enjoy pondering stone-age mysteries.

Fig. 7. (right) Mystery stones from Northern California.

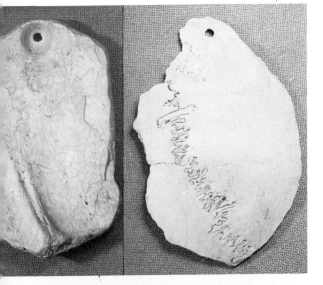

Fig. 8. (left) Gruesome twosome—bone pendants made by drilling fragments of human skulls.

Ducks and geese still return to Tule Lake, California. In the foreground can be seen the nettle plants used by the Indians for thread and cordage. The tules next to the edge of the water were used for basketry.

2. THE CANOE PEOPLE OF TULE LAKE

Land of the Burned-Out Fires

Mount Shasta, like most of the world's great mountains, has its share of legends and stories, but the beauty of its glacier-cut slopes and the impressive mass of the great peak distract the viewer from the mysteries that lie beyond. Few Californians know about the region of volcanoes, lakes, and caves which extends northeast into Siskiyou and Modoc counties. The National Park Service named it the "Land of the Burned-Out Fires."

Many crater-topped volcanic cones dot the area. In places, flows of lava have issued from the deep vents in the earth, building chimneys of stone around the openings. The flows from some are so recent that a virtual moonscape is visible. The molten material flowing toward the edge of Tule Lake Basin cooled on the surface and crusted over. The hot and softer interior lavas continued to flow, thus creating underground tube caves in an endless variety of shapes and contours. The entrance of one such cave is called Skull Cave (Fig. 9). Air currents in a few of the caverns have generated a temperature condition forming ice. One ice cave is named Frozen River, another Merrill's Ice Cave.

Some lava tubes have collapsed, producing a rough, block-like terrain. In other places, natural bridges remain to illustrate

Fig. 9. Skull Cave has a large diameter at the entrance. A river of ice is found in the lower region. (National Park Service photo).

Fig. 10. A portion of this collapsed lava tube remains to form a natural stone bridge. (Herald-News photo)

the structure of the former cave by showing it as a cross section (Fig. 10).

Cave Dwellers

It was only natural that the Indians would move into the protection of the structures so amply provided by the volcanic formations bordering the marshlands of Tule Lake. Some of the grottoes show extensive signs of occupation, but others little or none.

The juniper bark receptacle in Fig. 11 was left by one of the cave dwellers. Its construction is different from that of any other baskets of the hundreds observed. A long piece of juniper bark was evidently folded over when wet, and the sides were then laced together with tules. The curve, molded into the bottom of the container, provided a round shape for the upper portion and a surface on the lower part that would fit the knee of the owner. Even the red paint on the surface has been preserved by the dry condition in the rock cleft where it was found.

Water Craft of Tule Lake

The arid climate here is also responsible for the preservation of a cache of canoe paddles found about one-fourth mile from the lakeshore by Loren George (Fig. 12). A crack in the rocks provided a hiding place for the remains of a group of nine paddles, most of which were decomposed, though a few were surprisingly sound. The latter show fine workmanship. A midrib was carved up the center on each side. Designs, both painted and carved, displayed the artistry of the owner as he propelled his craft on the lake (Fig. 13).

There must have been hundreds of water craft of various types coursing upon Tule Lake because the number of stone boat anchors found there exceeds the total found at all other lakes in the region. Stone anchors such as those in Fig. 14 have become a virtual trademark in the farmyards and fence rows of the flat lake basin. The question arises as to what type of boat

Fig. 11. Well-preserved bark basket. Fig. 12. Canoe paddles from Tule Lake.

Fig. 13. The boatman decorated this paddle with a midrib, then painted and carved designs on both sides.

was used to encourage such widespread adoption of these anchors. On Upper Klamath Lake and Lower Klamath, the dugout canoe was standard equipment; however, there has never been a like abundance of boat anchors found at either of these watercourses. Also, Tule Lake is located at such a great distance from growing pine or fir trees that a transportation problem would discourage the widespread manufacture of canoes from logs.

The answer to the puzzle is perhaps to be found in the type of craft used by the neighbors of the Modoc in Nevada, the Washoe, who could quickly and easily make a boat of tules. The museum at Carson City, Nevada, contains an example of such a boat, along with the explanation of how the easily obtained tules were used to fashion it. The word raft probably better describes the type of boat. Bundles of the long, porous reeds were first bound together and then fashioned into a craft about three feet wide and eight feet long. This assembly of bundles was pointed on both ends for maneuverability. It floated in the water rather than upon it.

Whatever the name, this floating platform was very effective as a hiding place or blind to be used when trapping birds or fish. Pressure of the high winds against these floating bird blinds would require use of the large stone anchors. If one could have stood on the rocky ridge near Newell, California, several centuries ago, he would likely have seen these inland mariners on all sides of the lake.

Owls of Petroglyph Point

Today the wind-carved face of Petroglyph Point provides an excellent perching place for the owls that silently patrol the former campsites of the Modocs (Fig. 15). The owls that perch in these crevices, probably like all that have sat there in the centuries before them, seem oblivious to the land-bound people below. The owls are there for a purpose. Having no gizzard, they must wait for the strong juices of their digestive tracts to separate the hair and bones of their rodent victims from the sol-

Fig. 14. Typical heavy anchor stones.

Fig. 15. The winds have cut owl perches into the face of Petroglyph Point.

Fig. 16. Some designs etched into Petroglyph Point are similar to those along the Columbia.

Fig. 17. The volcano rim which forms Petroglyph Point can be more readily seen from a distance.

uble parts. After digestion is completed, they disgorge the furry pellets to the ground below, revealing the service they provide the farmers of the Tule Lake Basin.

Petroglyph Point, with its owls' perches, is part of the Modoc Lava Beds National Monument. Beneath these perches, and carved on the face of the cliff, are some of the most extensive and interesting prehistoric carvings in North America. For many centuries, the face of the cliff was protected from wind action because it was partially covered by the waters of Tule Lake. It must have been exposed at times, though, for the writings of the early lake dwellers appear for a quarter mile along the base of the hundred-foot cliff (Fig. 16). Some of the writings are high enough on the wall to have been made from canoes, while water was in the lake. Others were likely made during dry cycles under different geological conditions.

Actually the rock is the remains of an ancient volcano. The waters of Tule Lake have lapped against the wall of the old volcano until the west side is washed away and gives the appearance of having been sliced off with a giant knife. The remaining wall is made of a tan, semi-soft volcanic tuff resembling sandstone.

Remnants of the rim of the burned-out volcano cannot be seen from close up, but from a distance they show as a long peninsula extending into the lake from the east shore of Tule Lake (Fig. 17). On this vertical tablet of tuff the ancient artist tried to express himself. It is uncertain whether he had a message for others, or a prayer to offer in stone. Some of the carvings suggest a scoreboard. Possibly the soft stone face of the cliff was merely an ideal place for "doodling" with his stone tools.

The writings or markings of this region are of two types: petroglyphs, which are cut into the rocks; and pictographs, which are painted on the rocks. Although no word is decipherable, likely an effort was occasionally made to convey a message because both carvings and paintings have been used at some of the springs, burial places, and sacred places of the Indians. Pictographs are thought to have been used at Indian Wells Cave in the National Monument to indicate the presence of water.

The pictographs in Fig. 18 mark the entrance to a rock shelter on the west side of Tule Lake. In this picture, taken about fifty years ago, Captain O. C. Applegate, of Modoc War fame, was pointing out a particularly bright painting to A. M. Collier. Other cliffs and sites throughout the Klamath country and the deserts to the east bear inscriptions which seem to have no more relationship with existing objects than those at Petroglyph Point.

A short distance southwest from the point are ridges of broken gray rock where the great lava flows pushed into Tule Lake from the vent tubes of the Modoc Lava Beds (Fig. 19). In the distance tower the majestic heights of Mount Shasta.

Eight miles west of the sharp face of Petroglyph Point is Gillem's Bluff, where the United States Army camped during the Modoc Indian War. Northward, many miles of the nearly flat basin of Tule Lake stretch to the hills at Adams Point, across the state line into Oregon.

Crossroads of History

That such a remote, mysterious region should have played a significant part in the history of California and Oregon seems rather strange. The reason could lie in the geography of the area, for the low, level bed of Tule Lake would have provided a welcome alternative to the almost impassable barriers of lavas, mountains, and marshes to the west. The area became a natural crossroads for both primitive man and the white migrants who arrived later. Certainly the Klamath Indians from the north used this route on their way to capture slaves from the less aggressive Pit River Indians to the southeast; and the Modocs passed this way to gather salmon from the Klamath River and to raid their traditional enemies, the Shastas, who occupied the Klamath Canyon.

During a survey mission for the United States government, John Charles Fremont camped on the edge of Tule Lake, May 1,

Fig. 18. White, red, and black pictographs are pointed out by Captain O. C. Applegate and Andrew Collier for Burt Thomas, the photographer.

Fig. 19. Each chimney surrounds a vertical hole extending more than 100 feet into the earth.

1846. He named it Rhett Lake in honor of his friend, Barnwell Rhett of Charleston, South Carolina. Fremont later returned to participate in the Bear Flag Revolt. On this trip he was delayed at Tule Lake for three days because one of his hunters became lost. After that, he pushed on to the Klamath country, where he gave Lost River the name of McCrady River. Neither of his "names" survived.

A traveler who used the crossroads prior to Fremont was Peter Skene Ogden. He was the leader of a Hudson's Bay Company trapping and exploring expedition seeking furs, as well as a large river which supposedly flowed into San Francisco Bay. His party camped here in 1826. Ogden did not fare much better than Fremont in name-giving. He called present Tule Lake, Modoc Lake; and present Upper Klamath Lake, Dog Lake. However, he was successful in two major cases. He called the mountain "Sastise," after a tribe which his Modoc guides informed him occupied that area. Sastise has since been corrupted to Shasta. Ogden's "Pit River" has also survived the test of time as an official name for this stream in northeastern California. Pit River is additionally used as the unofficial name for the Indian tribe which occupied the valley of the river. These Indians, the Achomawi, spoke a variation of the Shasta language, but a decidedly different dialect than their neighbors on Hat Creek, the Atsugewi.

The misfortunes of the Hudson's Bay trappers, which led to the naming of Pit River, provide a colorful backdrop for the history of Modoc County. Ogden's first report on the Achomawi describes them as numerous, very wild, and uncommunicative. On May 7, 1827, however, a party of about twenty visited his camp. They warned his men to avoid the paths along the stream as they would encounter pits which had been dug to trap animals. Even with this advance warning, his men ran afoul of the cleverly concealed holes. Ogden wrote in his Journal on the same date: "Altho the Trappers were warn'd to avoid the Indian paths along the banks of the River—from the number of deep pits that they have made for entrapping wolves and deer—still three fell in with their horses. Two escaped fortunately without injury, but the third kill'd—a serious loss to his master. At the bottom of the pits a number of stakes are driven. The Natives inform us at times they kill a number of animals, some are nearly thirty feet deep."

In *Handbook of American Indians*, the purpose of the holes along the Pit River has been given as cooking or roasting pits. Ogden's Journal entry of May 10, 1827 dispels any doubt about the reason for the name: "It is almost incredible the number of pits the Indians have made along the River on both sides of the track as well as in it. They are certainly deserving of praise for their industry but from our not seeing the track of an animal I am not of opinion their labour is rewarded. From the number of pits—so as to warn others who may chance to travel in this quarter—I have nam'd this river Pit River. It is true we have lost a horse and a most valuable one and it is now almost surprising to me we have not lost more."

The trapping expedition moved north from near the present town of Canby, California, to the shores of Goose Lake, which they named Pit's Lake. By the spring of 1827, Ogden's descriptions of Indian life had become much less detailed. It is fortunate for historians that he had great interest in the habits and manner of dress of the Indians earlier, when he was at Tule Lake with the Modocs. His Journal entry on Christmas Day, 1826, contains this comment: "Six Indians paid us a visit. From their blankets being made of the feathers of ducks and geese, no doubt in the Fall and Spring there be vast quantities in this quarter. It cannot be otherwise there being so many lakes and the country low altho on both sides of us the mountains are very high, one in particular high above all others, pointed and well covered with snow." This was the peak he named Shasta.

Two days later, December 27, 1826, Ogden further noted: "We saw a Camp of Indians, in all men and women containing 60—the Clammittes (Klamaths) are far more numerous than I expected from the information I received at the Lake (Dog).

They had all blankets made of feathers and from a distance had rather a strange appearance. They are certainly entitled to some credit in devising such warm coverings."

Despite the carved records on Petroglyph Point, Ogden was the first to leave a clear written record of this important crossroads of history. From his high encampment, he could see Mount Shasta and was probably near the present southwest shore of Tule Lake. Some of his "Clammittes" doubtless lived under the cliff to the north.

Rock-Shelter Dwellers

The rock shelters along the cliff on the west side of Tule Lake were created when the lake was at a much higher level than during historic times. The overhang of the long fault was further undercut by the wave action of the water. This natural dwelling place was enhanced by the fact that the prevailing winds and rain from the west were cut off by the ridge. Fortunately for archeologists, the resulting dry conditions created a place where a more complete picture of the materials used by the Modocs would be preserved. In the open villages, the forces of decay, which consumed most things not made of stone or bone, were halted by the dry climate under the sheltering overhang.

It is fortunate that the caves preserved the material culture of the ancient Modoc inhabitants; otherwise, there would be meager knowledge of their way of life. One reason for the scarcity of information was the reluctance of any Modoc or Klamath Indian to mention the name of a person who had died. The Modocs could not pass along the tribal history without using the names of people. This taboo was encountered by Albert Gatschet who spent some time with the Klamaths and Modocs in 1888-89, as a representative of the United States Bureau of Ethnology. He wrote: "The Klamath people possess no historic traditions going further back in time than a century, for the simple reason that there was a strict law prohibiting the mention of a person or acts of a deceased individual by using his name.

This law was rigidly observed among the Californians (Modocs), no less than among the Oregonians, and on its transgression the death penalty could be inflicted. This is certainly enough to suppress all historic knowedge within a people."

The second reason for the failure of the Modoc and Klamath to retain knowledge or legends of migrations is the fact that they have occupied their present terrain for so many centuries. Some archeologists believe that the residents of the Klamath Highland may have come to the region from the desert to the east, possibly the Nevada area, around 7,500 years ago. Lacking history, names, or legends, the archeologist must put together such clues or leads as are available and compare them with the work of others, in an attempt to capture the true story of the prehistoric past.

The Age of Tules

The abundance of stones found on the old open campsites of the Modocs suggests that stone and bone were used exclusively by the former inhabitants. However, objects of wood, hide, and reeds would have disappeared through the weathering of the ages.

Clues from the dry-rock shelter show an entirely different picture. Here the objects of wood and basketry remain. The Age of Tules (or Reeds) would seem a more appropriate name than Stone Age. The tule was everything to the Klamaths and Modocs that the buffalo was to the Plains Indian; his clothing, his containers, his rafts, and his shelters were all made from this valuable marsh reed. Fig. 20 shows bundles of cattails which were stored for future use. The object below the bundles is a fire stick from the same shelter.

Two other components of the fire-making outfit are shown in Fig. 21. Both photos clearly reveal the holes burned at the point of friction. The lower stick appears to have been made from a broken bow. It was found on an open site by Audrey McPherson of Klamath Falls. These burned sticks are called "hearths" and

Fig. 20. Cattail bundles were stored for future use. The fire stick is burned on one end.

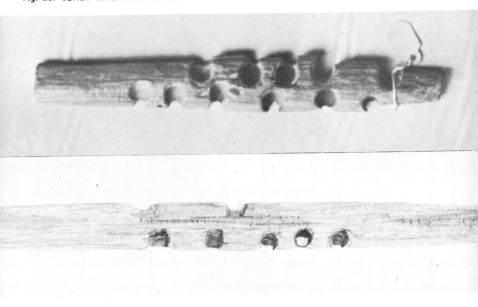

Fig. 21. Fire sticks or "hearths." The lower stick appears to have been made from a broken bow.

should give the modern Boy Scout assurance that his fire-making method is the authentic Indian style used by the Modoc.

Another use for the valuable tule plant is demonstrated in Fig. 22. This tule footwear from a rock shelter was donated to the Klamath County Museum by Joe Meeker. Colonel John C. Fremont reported that the Indians at the Klamath Marsh came to meet him wearing "grass shoes." They were very likely wearing shoes of this type stuffed with grass for insulation during the winter season. The loops at either side of the sole were probably tied at the top. For the cold winter climate of the Modoc homeland, such a shoe was far more practical than the buckskin moccasin, which would have been frozen stiff during most of the season.

Basketry

Basketry was the highest art medium for both the Modocs and their cousins, the Klamaths. The basket forms were, of course, adapted to the purpose served. Their many uses included: hats, storage baskets, winnowing shakers, "gathering" baskets, "burden" baskets, and cradleboards.

Mats and cooking baskets made up the greatest part of the household inventory. Fig. 23 illustrates three traditional basketry designs: on the left is the Arrow design; in the middle is the Quail or Quail Plume, which resembles the quail's tail; and on the right is the Lightning design, with a replica of "strikes of lighting."

The mat designs in the same photograph had no Indian name, but the two outer ones are currently called Herringbone by those who have studied basketry. These mats may have been made for the purpose of shaking the ground-seed of the water lily to separate the hulls, or they could have been used for gambling mats. Large tule and cattail mats served to cover the house floors, as well as the rafters of the winter house. Wren Frain, a Shasta Indian, explained to the writer that, in addition to mats, loose

Fig. 22. This tule sandal was easily insulated with grass or bark.

Fig. 23. Traditional basket designs: arrow, quail plume and lightning.

tules and cattails were sometimes laid on the rafters to help support the earth cover of the lodge.

Tules were plentiful, but the making of baskets was an arduous task. First came the gathering of the tules and then the splitting, which was done with a basketry awl. The damp, split portions were rolled into a double-twisted warp by a deft motion between the hand and thigh. After the reeds were prepared, the weaving could start.

Fig. 24 shows the hat style and the split-tule warp of the partly finished basket. The basketmaker is "Glass Eye," a Klamath woman. In both physical features and language, the Klamaths and Modocs were quite similar. This picture, from the Maude Baldwin collection in the Klamath County Museum, was taken about 1908. Besides what the picture says about basketry, it could carry other messages: the strong hands containing the skills for making a living; and the intense face reflecting concern over the problems of survival, or the lowly status of women—both conditions having prevailed in many primitive societies.

Because the harvesting of food might involve several miles of travel on foot, or a trip in a canoe, "carrying" or "burden" baskets were essential. Two types of burden baskets are shown in Fig. 25. The upper basket, made of split willow, has an unslit ring at the top. The lower one, held by Donelda DeVore, secretary at the Klamath County Museum, is made of split tule. Both are pointed at the lower end and were carried with a thong over the shoulder.

Food Storage and Cooking

During certain seasons of the year, there seemed to be no limit to the food which was available to the early inhabitants of Tule Lake. In the fall millions of waterfowl winged into the upland marshes. Even within the memory of the writer, these birds have been so numerous that their wings created a roar as they rose from the water. Because the presence of the waterfowl was seasonal, there was always the problem of storage—

Fig. 24. Basketmaker.

Fig. 25. Burden baskets.

Fig. 26. (below) Storage basket made of whole tules.

how to preserve the food so that a shortage could be avoided in the off seasons. Proper storage could well mean the difference between comfort and famine.

A porous basket of whole tules, loosely woven, was the most easily made and served the storage function best. Fig. 26 illustrates such a basket. The handle, though, likely shows the influence of white contact.

Porcupine quills, dyed yellow with lichens, were sometimes interwoven for decorative purposes. Although neither beads nor feathers were used as basket components in this area, Fig. 27 shows the use of the quills. They can be seen just above the heavy dark circle on the basket and just below it. The design on the mat in the figure, though a rather common one, was not given a name by the Modocs or the Klamaths. In the Southwest, however, Indians who used this design called it Squash Blossom.

When food was stored for a long time, it became quite dry and hard; therefore the roasting process was an unsuitable method of preparation. The cooking basket solved this problem. The food to be boiled was placed in a basket with water, then a hot rock was added by means of a forked stick. If one rock failed to complete the process, another replaced the original, and so on, until the desired results were achieved. This explains the large accumulation of seemingly useless rocks often found at the site of an Indian encampment.

Cooking rocks can usually be distinguished from other rocks by their jagged shape, or the dark color resulting from the burning process. In Fig. 28, the containers on either side are cooking baskets. The design on the left was called Crow's Knees, and the one on the right, Flying Bird. The basket in the center of the figure was made by the Shasta Indians. It shows the difference in the methods of ornamentation used by the Shasta women and the Modocs. The latter preferred a light background with a dark design, while the Shastas preferred to dye the tules in the background, leaving the undyed reeds for use in ornamentation. It

Fig. 27. Porcupine quills, dyed yellow, were used in this basket design.

Fig. 28. Shasta women made the darker basket in the center; Klamath cooking baskets flank it.

can be seen that the design patterns of the two tribes are quite similar.

The cradleboard in Fig. 29 is one of the few Modoc designs that did not resemble those of the Klamath; the Klamaths used a solid board with skin attachments to contain the baby. This split-willow cradle was identified from one illustrated by Stephen Powers in his report to the Bureau of American Ethnology in 1877. The mat beneath the cradleboard has the Trail design interwoven in the circles.

Early Modoc Report

The climate and terrain of the Modoc Country are described in an excellent firsthand account by Samuel Clark, war corre-spondent for the *New York Times* in 1873. During that year, Clark came to the Lava Beds region to observe and report the Modoc War. He wrote: "Take the Modoc country by itself and it must rank only to civilized life as an inhospitable region of alkali plains and barren hills, with no timber nearer than the surrounding mountains.

"Sagebrush and juniper scarcely vary the monotony; and the few meadow and swampland stretches that border the lake sides, and the emerald thread which occasionally marks with its winding path the course of some streamlet that seeks an outlet through the hills, all these are oases in the desert, and afforded camping places for the various Modoc bands when they located and made their permanent homes. . . . Modoc land, proper, in-cluded the alkali reaches of Little Klamath Lake, Tule Lake, Clear Lake, the circuit of Lost River, and the south shore of the Klamath River—where they met on a sort of neutral ground with their cousins and neighbors, the Klamaths.

"I have seen literally hundreds of old wickiup sites that were placed close together and evidently show the location of some great Indian town or village. . . . The shores of the Klamath are green and beautiful, and they may have been, long ago, the metropolitan seat of Modoc and Klamath commerce. The waters

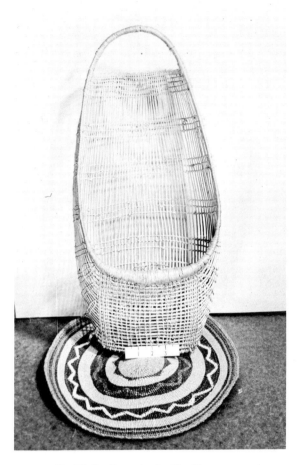

Fig. 29. Cradle made of split willow.

of the Klamath lakes have cut their way through the mountains and rush westward through dark canyons to the ocean. Klamath River empties the surplus waters of the Klamath Basin, but Clear Lake empties into Lost River, which winds among the hills making valleys along its way, then loses itself in Tule Lake. The remarkable fact is that while Lost River flows for a hundred miles from Clear Lake to Tule Lake, the two lakes are only five miles apart at the nearest point." (The distance is actually nine miles.)

The region may have seemed inhospitable to war correspondent Clark, but to the Modocs it offered an ideal combination of desert, lake, and marsh. The nearby ridges had some wild plums along the slopes, and the scabrock flats produced the ipo bulb, which resembles the dahlia bulb but is much smaller.

Deer Migration

One unusual and interesting feature of the environment of the Modocs is the migratory habit of the mule deer. Mount Shasta and the Cascade Range have created a high barrier for the clouds from the west; as a result, the area in and around the Lava Beds receives much less rainfall than the surrounding region. Each winter many deer from the north and east move out when the fall storms set in. Some deer come from a distance of more than eighty miles to pass the winter where the Mountain Mahogany, Bitterbrush, and Juniper grow in a virtually snow-free area. Their migratory pattern is said to be carried in the brains of the old does who lead the migrations. With this wintering habit, the deer were easily killed off and eventually were not easy for the Modocs to find. When they were found, they were used in their entirety: hide, horn, bone, and sinew. Even the hoofs were used—for rattles.

Hunting Methods

With whole villages to be supplied, it was necessary to procure food in large quantities. Ordinary hunting methods were supplemented by the use of traps, wiers, and blinds. For many types of animals the bow and arrow were also used.

A unique type of arrow was employed for shooting at a flock of birds on the water. It was tipped with a fire-hardened wooden point. The arrow had a ring of pitch about an inch back from the point of the foreshaft. This ring caused the arrow to skip along on the water at the proper level to make connection with the sitting birds. In this way the hunter solved half of his accuracy problem. The water served as a guide for the arrow as it skipped along, and he had only to get the flock on target from a horizontal position.

Fig. 30, No. 3, shows such an arrow. Time has removed most of the pitch but the ring is easily apparent. No. 1 shows a long, wooden foreshaft which has been bound to a shaft of cane. The broken obsidian point has been bound with sinew. No. 6 is a shaft of cane pointed with a fire-hardened wooden point, attached with a fiber that resembles hemp. Nos. 5 and 7 are pieces of cane shaft with sinew wrapping. No. 4 is a wooden foreshaft with a fragment of an arrowhead attached.

A native cane provided the most popular material for arrow-shafts. An arrowhead attached directly to the main shaft would seem like the simplest and most logical way of mounting the point, but this was not the pattern used when cane shafts were prepared. Instead of mounting the shaft to the cane portion, the Modoc workman used a wooden foreshaft. Often the preferred method of mounting was a wooden nock for seating the bow-string in the back of the arrow. This pattern of arrow construction was also found to be prevalent in the caves to the east. Fig. 31 shows such a wooden point and nock from a Warner Valley cave.

An inexhaustible supply of obsidian for the making of arrow points was available to the Modocs at nearby Glass Mountain. The volcanic glass flow is about nine miles south and east of Petroglyph Point on the northeast side of the mountain. Here a

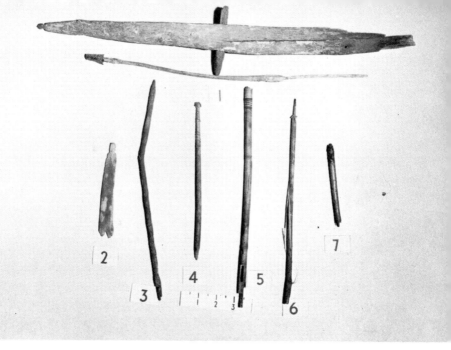

Fig. 30. Bow and arrow fragments.

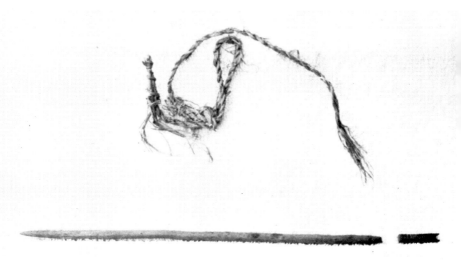

Fig. 31. This wooden point and nock were once wrapped to a shaft of native cane.

long cliff of broken obsidian blocks can be seen more than two miles long, and in places over three hundred feet thick.

Evidence indicates that the arrow makers and traders sat around the base of the cliff to chip large flakes or spalls from the glassy stone. These they shaped into large, crude blades called "blanks." In this form the material was easy to transport and ready for further shaping into tools or weapons.

A study of the Glass Mountain flow was made by C. W. Chesterman of the University of California. He determined by carbon 14 dating of ancient tree trunks that the volcanic activity took place about six hundred years ago. Since flakes of obsidian from this source are identifiable on many archeological sites in California and Oregon, the material provides a method of determining an age limit of six hundred years.

Archeological studies have revealed that the bows all seem to be much smaller than those in use by Indians of historic times. The pull would be much less and may account for the popularity of the light cane arrowshaft. The bow fragment pictured at the top of Fig. 30 was found imbedded in a heavy bank of peat in Lower Klamath Lake. Because the peat acted as a preservative, only the protruding portions were decayed. The back of this bow seems scratched as though it might have been backed by sinew. No. 2 in Fig. 30, a small fragment, compares in size with those found in the Payne collection in the Klamath County Museum. In Fig. 32, a close-up of the arrow illustrates the method of attachment with sinew.

Applegate Party Opens the Modoc Country

The name of Applegate has greatly enriched both the history and the geographical names of Oregon. Like Ogden and Fremont before them, members of the Applegate Party passed through the crossroads north of Petroglyph Point. These pioneers from the Willamette Valley were seeking a route into Oregon that would be free from jeopardy by the British on the Columbia and, if possible, provide a shorter and more easily traveled route from

Fig. 32. This obsidian arrow point was wrapped onto the wooden foreshaft with animal sinew.

Fig. 33. Volcanic holes and fissures made natural fortifications for Jack's band of Modocs. (Herald-News photo)

Fort Hall, into the Willamette Valley. The trail which was successfully established became known as the Southern Route to the Oregon Trail. The old road passed along the north edge of Tule Lake and provided a crossing of Lost River on a rock ledge called the Natural Bridge. (It was actually an underwater ford.)

The opening of the Southern Route by the Applegate Party provided the Modocs with a ready source of goods, which was almost unbelievably easy to acquire. The temptation to take it was too much for those whose teeth were worn flat from eating the tough and sinewy winter meat of the mule deer, and whose cooking pots never lost the taste of the meal before. As the wagon trains of the pioneers descended the slopes on the east shore of the lake in 1888—still called by Ogden's name of Modoc Lake—they were easy prey for the native warriors. The name Bloody Point preserves the memory of the attacks; and the trail, eroded where the wagon wheels cut the surface, is still visible in many places—but the graves of the victims are unmarked.

The Modoc War

The Applegate expedition also focused attention on the grassy meadows along the north shore of Tule Lake. The more adventuresome pioneers soon started utilizing these ranges and establishing homes there. During that time, many Modocs were attracted by the good life offered in the gold-mining camps around Yreka. Despite this diversion and income, the inevitable conflict between settlers and natives occurred, with the pioneers demanding that the Indians be removed to the Klamath Reservation in northern Klamath County. Their demands were met and the Indians were relocated.

The Modocs at Yainax, near the present town of Sprague River, were able to make a satisfactory adjustment to living with their Klamath cousins, but those at Modoc Point were soon dissatisfied; and under the leadership of Kintpuash, Captain Jack, they returned to their ancient refuge near Petroglyph Point. Such defiance of federal orders brought immediate action to return the

Fig. 34. Rough terrain provided natural shelter, and limited rainfall made the Lava Beds a good place to winter. (Herald-News photo)

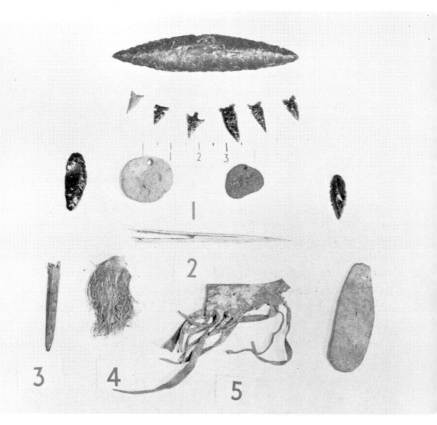

Fig. 35. Chipped objects and specimens from a rock shelter.

fugitives. This, in turn, caused Jack's band to retreat into the lunar-like landscape of the Lava Beds (Figs. 33 and 34). From this maze of twisted stone, hidden caves, lava flows, and natural trenches, the Modocs brought on one of the most unusual and costly wars in the history of the United States Army. More than two hundred white soldiers and volunteers from Yreka, California, and Jacksonville, Oregon, were killed, while only thirteen Modocs lost their lives.

Government of the Indian

Captain Jack's band did not include all Modocs, as the Modocs were not a nation as we understand it . . . San Francisco is different from Oakland, and both differ from Portland. All three, however, are served by a national government of similar structure. This has given the citizens of every city in the United States a national heritage as well as a local heritage. But such was not the case with the Modocs. The loose territorial agreement that was worked out by the Modocs and Klamaths did not mean that either group was a united nation. There were still occasional forays against the territory of the neighboring tribe, as well as revenge and plunder raids between villages within the tribes.

Among both the Modocs and Klamaths, the village group was of much greater importance than the nation, since it concerned the way of life of both the family and the individual. Living habits and group migrations often varied more from village to village than from tribe to tribe. A Modoc village with a desirable fishing site, or one near a wocas patch, could resemble Klamaths more in their way of life than even other Klamaths. In general, though, the Modocs moved around more with the seasons to harvest certain berries and roots. Also, the migration of the deer herds affected their movement more than it did the less mobile Klamaths. The Snakes, who lived in the territory bordering the Klamaths and Modocs on the east, were even less stable than either. They moved with the seasons, living in permanent quarters only in winter.

The territorial agreement between the Modocs and the Klamaths occasionally went even further, developing into a joint military operation. If the Snakes, Umpquas, or Shastas became involved in a raid on the territory of either, the Lutuami-speaking groups might call their neighbors to join them for defense or revenge. Both the Klamath and Modoc groups also kept a continual pressure on surrounding tribes by enslavement and attrition. When the United States Government assumed authority over these people, it encouraged the selection of a single chief or leader, in order to avoid doing business with the various village leaders who were recognized as sub-chiefs.

Change in Shore Lines

It is easy to see the contour of this Indian country from the top of Sheepy Ridge. The basin, almost as flat as a floor, slopes gently to the south. At the beginning of the historic period, the water was about twenty-five feet deep at the edge of the Modoc Lava Beds. The old beach is well marked by signs in the monument at the place where the trail to Captain Jack's stronghold enters the lavas. The various levels are also well marked by water stains along the wall at Petroglyph Point. The shore was steep at the south end, and as the lake level changed the new shore was only a few feet from the old beach.

On the north end of the lake, however, the effect was different: there the land sloped gently, and a variation of a few inches in the depth of the water produced considerable change in the shore line. Through the ages, the camps of the Modocs shifted with this shore. During wet periods the Indians would retreat as far as Adams Point.

As they moved with the weather cycles, they left many remains of their material culture at the old beach levels. At the top of Fig. 35 is shown the knife and the type of arrowheads used. The line below shows two disk-shaped, stone net weights, which are unusual in this region. The items in the lower two rows are from a rock shelter and include the end of a fire-hard-

Fig. 36. Bedrock mortar holes provided a place for visiting as well as for grinding food.

Fig. 37. (below) Birds, bulbs, and insects from a rock shelter.

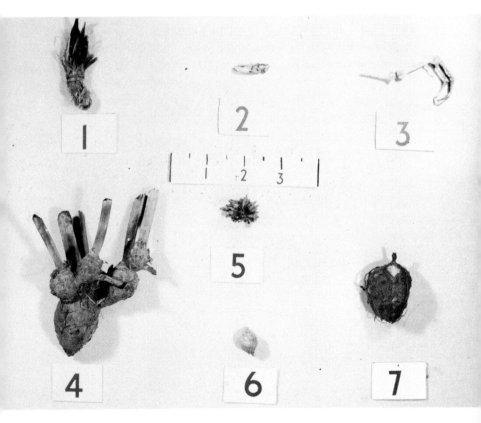

ened stick (No. 3). A wooden paddle appears at the right. The plant root bundle (No. 4) had been stuffed with cattail down. No. 2, a crane's beak, could very well be the remains of a roasted crane dinner. No. 5 is a piece of buckskin fringe which is stiff and more like rawhide.

Life in an Ancient Rock Shelter

There are many mortars remaining in the bedrock below the rock shelters, along the west shore of Tule Lake. One rock contains a number of such pits (Fig. 36). It does not require a great imagination to recreate a scene from the past along the old shore. Here the women sat in the warmth of the rising sun from the east, grinding their food, evaluating their menfolk, or complaining about the scarcity of deer sinew. Keeping the children out of the canoes and the dogs away from the roasting food would be a never-ending task. Some of the large rocks have been worn completely through by the pestles the busy women used.

The task of supplying food, as well as preparing it, fell heavily upon the females of the tribe. Some examples of the menu available are pictured in Fig. 37. No. 1, a bundle of mallard feathers wrapped with tules, shows that after the bird was eaten, his plumage may have been used for a paintbrush. No. 2, a dried grasshopper, and No. 3, the dried foot of a perching bird, illustrate other animal foods. The bulbs (Nos. 4, 5, 6, and 7) are not the usual ones included in the Modoc diet.

Generations of Indian maidens were undoubtedly reared in the rock shelters below Sheepy Ridge and trained in the arts of survival. Probably most young males with marriage in view would give as much consideration to the bride's ability to catch and prepare a meal, as they would to her grace as a dancer or to the beauty of her eyes. Another factor which must have entered into the shaping of a romance was the condition of the prospective bride's teeth. Fig. 38 shows a number of fiber bundles probably used in making basketry or cordage. All seem to have been chewed. Beautiful teeth indeed!

Fig. 38. Chewed fiber bundles.

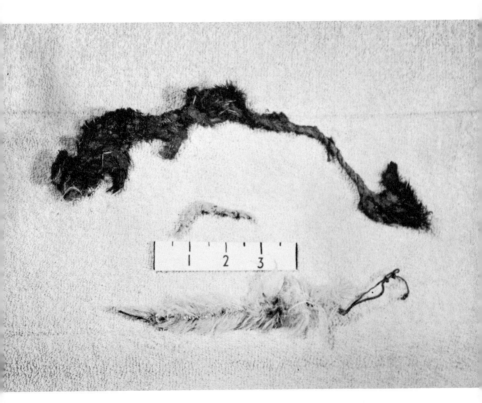

Fig. 39. Feather cloth materials.

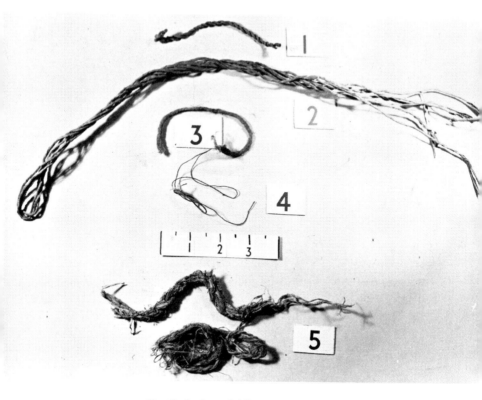

Fig. 40. Cordage of different sizes and materials.

The materials in Fig. 39 give clues to the method used in making the feather blankets described by Peter Skene Ogden. The black, twisted bird skin, at the top, appears to be that of a coot. In the lower part of the picture are white duck feathers which have been twisted into a cord of nettle fiber forming a bangle. The small piece of weasel skin in the center appears to have been dried rather than tanned.

Since the welfare of the family depended considerably upon the fishing, netting, trapping, and shooting of game, the need for good cordage and string was great. The Modocs used a variety of plants for this purpose. Fig. 40 illustrates several types and sizes of cordage. No. 1 is of tule, twisted for basketry. No. 2 is also tule but prepared differently, as though for a rope. No. 3 is a large-gauge nettle fiber cord. No. 4 is a nettle fiber but very finely twisted and hard to distinguish from modern cotton string. The large cords, No. 5, are of sagebrush bark and, although quite brittle now, would have served as useful rope when originally made. The fiber of native iris and a plant called Indian hemp were also used for cordage.

If it is hard for us today to understand the social customs and living patterns of the early Indians, it was difficult for them to understand the strange values of the white man. And, if the female seemed to carry more than her share of the work load, she also realized her importance and value. This can best be illustrated by a story told to the writer by the late Judge U. E. Reeder, who came early to Lake and Klamath counties. An old-timer, Reeder had a friend named Jake, who was married to an Indian woman. On his infrequent trips to town, Jake would usually succumb to his fondness for alcoholic liquors. His helpless condition and flat wallet were naturally deplored by his Indian wife. On one occasion following a bout with John Barleycorn, Jake was confronted by a more than usually angry spouse. As he staggered in, she was heard to comment:

"You no good. You no good for nothing" — and finally the crowning insult, "White woman good enough for you."

Table Mountain and the ridge extending toward the south divide Silver Lake Basin from Christmas Lake Valley. Picture Rock Pass into Summer Lake is only a short distance from this ridge.

3. THE DESERT

Table Mountain is an almost perfect mesa. Located northeast of Silver Lake bed in northern Lake County, it forms a part of Picture Rock Pass between Silver Lake Valley and Summer Lake Valley.

Of Picture Rock Pass, Lewis McArthur notes in *Oregon Geographic Names*: "The name comes from some strange designs of pictures on the rocks about a hundred feet south of the highway. These peculiar marks, made by Indians, are strongly suggestive of a WPA painting project operated by the aborigines." Throughout the sagebrush region of central and southwest Oregon, there are many groups of such pictures, some of which suggest real sign writing.

The sides of Table Mountain slope up symmetrically until the brown sandy soil reaches the rimrock which forms the table. The rise then becomes a vertical cliff with a level top. One who sees Table Mountain need not be told its name. The mountain is interesting in itself from the standpoint of both beauty and geology. It is the country surrounding the mountain, however, that is most interesting.

This is Snake Indian country—the Oregon Desert. At least the Snakes lived here at the time of exploration by white men.

51

This large linguistic group is called both Shoshonean and Paiute by the scientists, but trappers and Indians referred to this group as the Snakes. Flanked by the Klamaths on the west, they spread north toward the Columbia and ranged into Idaho, Nevada, Utah, and parts of California. The remnants of one group, in Northern California, are called the Surprise Valley Paiutes.

From the top of Table Mountain, several areas of Snake habitat are visible. To the southeast lies Summer Lake, named by Fremont, whose party was cheered by the sight of the warm springs. Anna River at the north end is the chief source of water for Summer Lake. Arising entirely from springs, this stream is a wonder to geologists as there is not enough rainfall in the entire adjacent area to provide the flow which Anna River produces. The only explanation for the volume seems to be that the water must travel in a subterranean stream from the Cascade Mountains underneath another range of mountains to appear again in Summer Lake Valley.

Silver Lake and the former Paulina Marsh are due west of Table Mountain. During wet-weather cycles, these bodies of water must have provided a welcome oasis for the desert-dwelling Snakes. The shores of both bodies of water bear evidence of intensive occupation. The former camps are marked by thousands of flakes of obsidian and the smaller triangular arrowheads which identify these Shoshonean people.

One of the periodic dry-weather cycles occurred in the area during the 1930s. As rainfall was reduced, the water became lower and warmer. Evaporation exceeded inflow and the entire region was deprived of its cover of water. Valley ranchers were quick to take advantage of the fertile new soil, but their grain drills opened the humus-laden soil to the dry winds blowing across the Cascade Range. These winds soon changed the lake basin and former marsh into a dune-pocked desert. Sand accumulated so rapidly at the old U R ranch at the east end of the lake that a horse team and "fresno" scraper were required to keep the

Fig. 41. Sand and tumbleweed have encroached on this desert cabin.

Fig. 42. A former home yields to
the wind.

road open. (The "fresno" is a one-handled, wide, shallow scoop with steel runners to help raise the load for hauling and dumping.) When this work became a losing battle with the elements, the highway was raised in order to keep the road open toward Lakeview.

The blowouts on the dried beds of the lake and marsh finally revealed the remains of a civilization which had once lived there but had disappeared long before the Snake chiefs led their people into the Silver Lake Valley.

Ghost Farms of the Fort Rock Area

While the ancient fossils and artifacts of the Silver Lake bed were being uncovered, the three producers of erosion—drought, wind, and plow — were blowing away the hopes of the homesteaders who had settled in the nearby desert valleys. The soil, so productive that it grew giant sagebrush, was dependent upon the native cover for its stability. Planting time became the season of the "blows." Without moisture or cover, the soil started to move. Occasionally the buildings of the pioneers were filled with the soil from their own fields, as shown in Fig. 41.

A few homesteaders such as Henry Hatch and Archie Warner stayed to battle the elements. There was still a school, a store, and a post office at the town of Lake (near the present site of Christmas Lake) when we first visited the area; however, the post offices at Fleetwood, Arrow, and Connley were gone. Fences were down, sand dunes bordered the fields, and a few cattle picked at the bits of grass on lands then owned by Lake County because of delinquent taxes.

Where the soil blew out from beneath the abandoned houses, sometimes a baby shoe, a broken doll's head, or a purple castoria bottle would serve as a reminder of the hopes of the family that had once occupied the now-deserted ruins. The tilt of the building depended on the direction of the wind currents. (Fig. 42).

Frontier Social Center

We were fortunate in being able to visit the friendly town of Silver Lake before the age of gasoline had completely replaced the culture of the "hay burner" period of horses. During the days of freight teams the town was a thriving village. It provided a way point on the freight routes and a business center for the cattlemen and homesteaders whose houses dotted the nearby foothills and low sandy ridges toward the east. Horse travel made the early hotels social centers as well as profitable enterprises. With a horse you could get to town but time would not permit a return trip the same day.

When we first started visiting the Silver Lake country, there were no freight teams left and little horse travel except for an occasional cowboy. There were still two hotels in the town, the Chrisman and the Silver Lake Hotel, but we made little use of these hotels. Our preference—except in early spring—was camping out on the desert, either near an abandoned homesteader's cabin or in a protected gulley. In early spring, icy winds coming directly from the snow-covered Cascades made sleeping out rather uncomfortable.

The Chrisman Hotel was operated by the genial host Ed Lundy and his wife. The food was good and the rooms satisfactory. Each room had its own heating system: a sheet-iron stove which guests could fire to suit their individual needs, depending upon how hard the wind was blowing. Good, clean water could be found in the pitchers on the stand and the sewer system was located under the bed.

One of the things I liked best about the Chrisman was the system the management used to encourage the guests to go to sleep. During the early evening hours, the hum of the gasoline-driven electrical system could be heard. The single bulb lighting fixture gave out an adequate, if somewhat changeable glow. When the time for sleep arrived, the noise of the motor would stop and the lights would go out for the night. The Lundys were considerate people and I am sure there must have been a scheduled time to turn off the motor. Since we did not stay often enough to learn the schedule, it was interesting to guess when the moment for darkness would come.

My wife enjoyed the luxury of sleeping inside but was always anxious about the hotel catching on fire with so many stoves in use. I assured her that, in case of fire, one could easily leap from the window and suffer, at the most, a broken leg or sprained ankle. Actually both hotels did eventually burn, first the Silver Lake and then the Chrisman.

We usually arrived in the Silver Lake country when the town was celebrating Saint Patrick's Day; March 17 was about the time the sands of the lake bed were sufficiently dry to start the creeping movement that often uncovered the obsidian and fossil-bone implements of the old villages.

Our initial trip to Silver Lake was memorable. We had gone to the Fort Rock area in two cars for a combination deer and arrowhead hunt. After a hot day of fruitless searching for both in the area north of Connley Hills, we decided to break into two parties, one for deer, the other to hunt artifacts on the dry shores and bed of Silver Lake. I voted to stay with my wife and her mother at the lake. The rest of the party, led by Mr. Reeder, headed from our camp on Buck Creek for Hager Mountain.

Our efforts brought little result. There were numerous flakes of obsidian and some broken rocks but few of the pieces could be considered "keepers." The sandy condition of the lake bed prevented our driving very far into the flat expanse, so we walked along, rather aimlessly. An occasional piece of obsidian encouraged us to continue. Branching out on my own, I found a large arrowpoint, my best up to that time. Other broken fragments and camp rocks soon appeared on the blown-out places of the dry lake bed. Then it was not long before I had found eight or ten creditable arrowpoints, also the matching halves of a broken knife nearly six inches long.

At about this time I looked up from the ground long enough to see my wife wildly gesturing for me to come. Reluctantly, be-

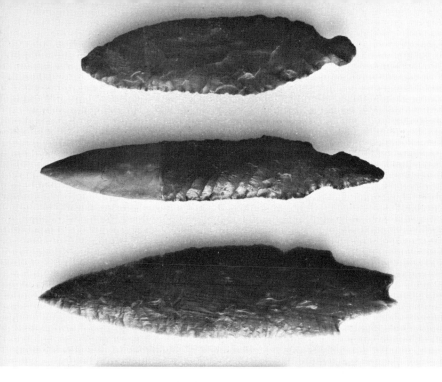

Fig. 43. Broken spears with unusual backs.

Fig. 44. A thin Silver Lake broad point.

cause I was having some luck, I· broke the pattern of my search in order to join her, about a half mile away. I found more points on the way. I expected her to suggest that we give up and leave, but instead she told me of finding a pocketful of fine points and a fossilized bone needle. She had the thrilling experience of picking up twenty-five points as fast as she could move from one to another. Among her treasures was the back end of a spearhead, so unusual in color and shape that we valued it highly even though the point was broken from it. The spear showed beautiful chipping, and when we held it to the light, darker stripes were visible.

Two years later, while we were hunting in the same area of the lake bed, a "Believe It Or Not" occurred. Where winds had blown the sands away, I found the point of a spearhead which I felt must be the point from our broken spear. It had the same fine workmanship and the darker bands running through the obsidian. Proof, of course, had to wait for matching the two pieces of the gray blade. When this was done, we found that the two pieces fitted exactly. There was no doubt that we had the missing point. The complete spear is shown at the bottom of Fig. 43. In the center is another broken spearhead with such an unusual point of attachment that I could not resist making a clay point to complete it. At the top is another of the points I restored from the original parts.

The sands of Silver Lake bed yielded very different pieces from the type we had expected. They had allowed us to peer through the mists of time but, in doing so, had created as many mysteries as were solved. In the blowouts, an Indian culture very different from that of the Paiutes was revealed, but we may never find out why the artifacts from the eroded areas in the middle of Silver Lake vary so much from those of the surrounding area. The answer might lie in the uses to which tools were put or to the time in which the lake-bed dwellers lived. From several years' study I have learned that projectile points vary so much individually that a single point will not give a sound clue to its

Fig. 45. Willow-leaf knives were unusually abundant on Silver Lake.

Fig. 46. (below) Unusual material, plus fine workmanship.

location. However, an examination of many of them will usually reveal a pattern that indicates where such an artifact was probably found.

At Silver Lake the points are larger than those found at most other sites. Fig. 44 shows a wide piece, probably too heavy to have been used as a dart with an atlatl. Its general shape is that of a spear. At the same site in the deep stratum of the old lake bed, an abundance of willow-leaf-shaped knives was also found. Most of these (Fig. 45) are of obsidian, but some are of jasper and chert. The colors of gray, pink, and yellow do not show in black and white photography but the workmanship is brought out in Fig. 46. The center knife, 8¼ inches long, appears to have been resharpened by its owner, who had flaked one end to a narrow point.

Fossil-Bone Artifacts

Another odd feature of the lake-bed culture is the fossilized condition of the bone artifacts. All the ancient ones seem to have turned to stone. This was not true of those recently deposited, but the ones which had been fashioned by the Indians were definitely fossilized. Whether this condition was due to the great age of the specimens or to the mineral content of the lake waters is unknown.

A great variety of pieces from the lake bed is represented in Fig. 47. The three fragments in the upper center are beveled at one end and resemble the projectile points from Lower Klamath Lake. The long point in the center is not beveled on the back end but, instead, comes to a conical point. The vertical piece above No. 2 is definitely a short, beveled, fossil-bone point. The two short, notched specimens could be either harpoon points or projectile points.

Possibly these smaller notched points were not even made by the ancient residents of the Silver Lake area. Herman Robe, a former employee of the Oregon Museum of Natural History, told the writer of a Canadian goose killed about the year 1915, near

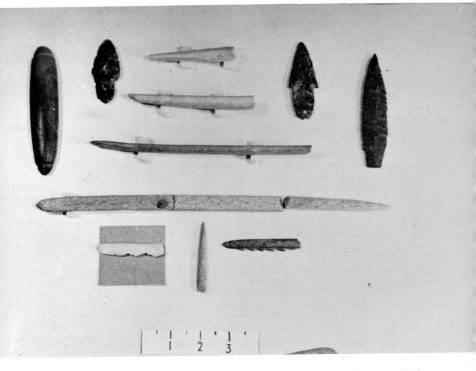

Fig. 47. The upper bone pieces have been beveled as though for mounting on a shaft.

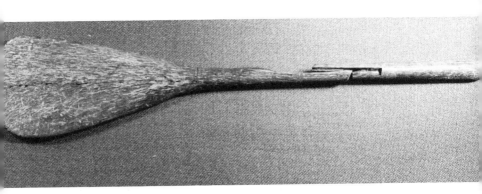

Fig. 48. Fossilized bone paddle.

Brownsville, Oregon. Clarence Templeton, who killed the goose, found imbedded near its wing a point of bone resembling a harpoon. The Alaskan or Canadian hunter who fired the point into the goose could have had predecessors whose harpoons were left on the bed of Silver Lake in the same manner. The scarcity of this harpoon-type artifact suggests that they were rarely used.

The obsidian projectile points in Fig. 47 are the proper size for dart points. In the upper left is a nicely finished atlatl weight.

The channel entering Silver Lake from the north end is called Reeder Slough, after the homesteaders who settled there. Actually it was an extension of the Paulina Marsh, named for Chief Paulina of the Snake band. The culture at the bottom of Reeder Slough resembled that on the lake bottom. The stone and bone elements were not just those shot or dropped there by people from the shore. All the stone components of a complete camp were present: mortars and metates (vessels for grinding), pestles and manos (handstones for grinding), mauls (Indian hammers), and even one tubular pipe. Most of the stones were broken but they were found in sufficient quantity to indicate that they had been used on the site. It is likely that, during a dry weather cycle, a marsh existed here for a considerable period to allow for the accumulation of so many stones.

The bone paddle, Fig. 48, had been about ten inches long before it was broken. The bone is from a fairly good-sized animal, but the animal is unidentifiable. It is also not known whether the bone was fossilized before the paddle was made or turned to stone after being lost in the camp where it was discovered. The four spoon-shaped objects to the left, in the top row of Fig. 49, were found in Christmas Valley. All were uncovered by wind action on the valley floor, and none were fossilized. The two in the center have pointed handles which indicate that they were used for a second purpose, that of a punch. The other spoon-like objects in this figure are from the bed of Lower Klamath Lake, but none compare in quality with the fossil paddle from the Sil-

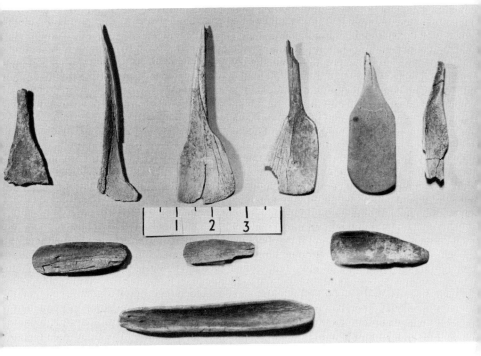

Fig. 49. Types of bone spoons or scoops.

Fig. 50. Crude stone weights.

ver Lake bed. The latter could have been a shaman's tool, so finely is it decorated.

Sinkers and Hot Rocks

There seems to be no native stone on the Silver Lake bed and the only rocks found there had been carried to the site by the Indians. Two types of stone artifacts, though, were especially abundant. One was the crudely made stone weights shown in Fig. 50. These rocks had a groove cut around them as though for holding a thong. They could have been used as net weights by the fishermen of the Snake Tribe—or as part of the camping equipment of the more ancient people who lived there prior to the Snakes.

The second type of stone artifact found here in great numbers —and to a lesser extent in all of the old camps of the Klamath country—is shown in Fig. 51. One Indian said that these flat stones were "hot rocks" for cooking. There are several reasons for my belief that the stones must have had a different purpose: first, they are too thin to convey much heat; second, they are too numerous on some lake beds where no camp exists; and third, many are notched on the side as though to allow for the attachment of a string or handle. A number of uses other than cooking have been suggested for these stones; they could have been wocas spoons, clam crackers, or net weights. The last explanation seems logical as they are found in great numbers where waterfowl and fish could have been netted.

A Famous Site for Ancient Man

From the top of Table Mountain looking north, it is possible to see the part of Fort Rock Valley containing the historic landmark of Fort Rock. This interesting formation served not only as a point of scenic interest but for a more practical purpose. U. E. Reeder, who rode for cows here, told how a single cowboy could hold an entire herd of cattle within the semicircular walls of Fort Rock simply by patrolling the open end of the steep enclosure.

Fig. 51. Thin, worked stones are found on many sites.

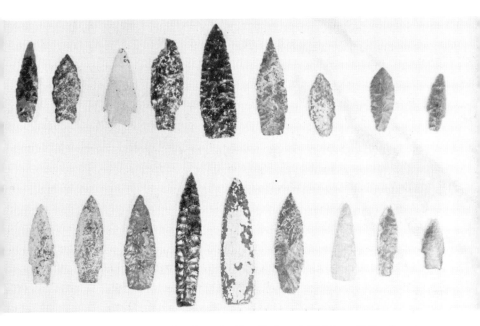

Fig. 52. All these points were found on the Fort Rock and Christmas Valley Desert—except the black point in the bottom row. This one, a Yuma type, is from Silver Lake.

The rock and adjacent land have been granted to the government as a state park by Mr. Reub Long.

A nearby cave has proved to be the point of one of America's most significant archeological discoveries. In this cave a number of sagebrush sandals were discovered by a party from the University of Oregon Department of Anthropology. The sandals lay beneath the pumice of the eruption of Mount Mazama. Testing by means of the Carbon 14 method proved that the sandals were around 9,000 years old. The well-developed basketry techniques strongly suggested that the sandal wearers must have been here for a considerable time prior to this, in order to have had time to invent and improve the methods of basket manufacture.

East of Table Mountain in Christmas Valley, upon the remains of ancient Indian campsites and abandoned homesteads, another group of occupants is presently establishing itself; a source of electrical power enables these new settlers to utilize the underground water. It was in this same valley at Fossil Lake that Oregon's pioneer geologist, Dr. Thomas Condon, made what is probably the first observations by a scientist on the ancient people of this desert. On the blown-out bed of Fossil Lake, he found their projectile points in association with fossil bones. With true scientific skepticism, he wrote: "The mixture of these artifacts may be due entirely to the simple law of gravitation, for both arrowpoints and recent shells have been settled down among the fossils as the dust and sand upon which they rested was gradually blown away."

Here, too, Condon found the bones of gulls, cormorants, and flamingos, as well as those of camels, horses, and elephants. Perhaps under the sand also lie the bones of one of these pleistocene mammals holding the dart points of its ancient hunter. The plow of one of the new settlers in Christmas Valley may turn up what has been missed before.

Before the Bow and Arrow

The projectile points in Fig. 52 were found in Fort Rock Valley and eastward in Christmas Valley. The men who made and used them lived here before the Paiutes brought their bows and small triangular arrows—and during a much wetter period. During post-glacial times, the present-day ridges enclosed lakes and ponds. The water provided greater variety of fauna and flora, as well as greater abundance of both. The projectile points are too heavy to make good arrowpoints; they were very likely points for darts which were propelled by means of an atlatl. They are too heavy for the bow, too small to be considered knives. The close-up in Fig. 53 shows the typical broad base, the fine workmanship, and the accumulation of mineral salts which the ages have attached to them.

The atlatl is a spear thrower which serves as an extension of the human arm. Though it was invented centuries before the bow and arrow, there is proof in some cases that the latter were employed during the same time as the atlatl. The atlatl was much less accurate as a weapon, and much harder to use. The length of the atlatls found in Oregon varies from about twenty to twenty-seven inches. Each spear thrower had notches or holes to fit the fingers and a handle to grasp. The spear or dart was laid upon the thrower with the hollowed nock fitted into a hook of either wood or stone similar to those shown in Fig. 54. The hook on the right in the figure is made of a white stone with decorative grooves at the back. The point slopes like that in the drawing. It has been positively identified by two professional archeologists. The hook on the left is made of green jade. Both specimens are from Clear Lake. However, more wooden hooks or spurs have been found than stone ones; the latter may have been used to replace one on a damaged atlatl.

The finding of broken hooks shows that considerable force was exerted in the process of throwing the dart. The hunter propelled the dart by making an over-hand motion. The length of the atlatl allowed the thrower to develop a greater velocity than he could with his arm alone; also to use a heavier projectile point than the bow.

The stones in Figs. 55 and 56 are called atlatl weights. It has

Fig. 53. These mineral-encrusted points are believed to be very old.

Fig. 54. (below) Stone atlatl spurs were pointed to engage the hollowed shaft of the dart.

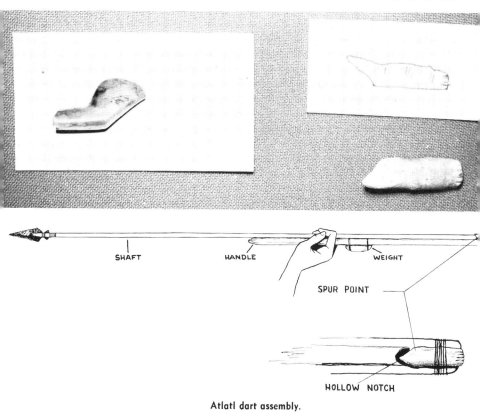

SHAFT   HANDLE   WEIGHT

SPUR POINT

HOLLOW NOTCH

Atlatl dart assembly.

been only in recent years that proof as to their use was established by the finding of atlatls with the weights attached. Prior to this, they were sometimes called plummets, ceremonial stones, or measuring stones. The stones differ in shape but all have two characteristics in common: a flat or slightly concave surface for seating on the wooden back of the stick, and a groove or hole cut in one or two places to receive the string which fastened them to the atlatl. Most of them had a rounding, loaf-shaped back which might have been shaped to fit between the fingers. These weights have not been found in great quantity, but they have appeared over a wide area.

The Paiute Way of Life

Both ancient man and the Paiute, who moved into his habitat, were taxed to the utmost to survive in the usually dry valleys of their range. The slopes of the hills were clad with scattering junipers, but the valley floors were devoid of any large trees. The ravens have taken advantage of the juniper tree which made the mistake of growing away from its kind on the Fort Rock Desert (Fig. 57). From the size of the nest it appears that many generations of the shiny black stick-collectors have been reared in it.

One of the few plants which could thrive on the dry valley floors in eastern Oregon was artemesia, commonly called sagebrush. Today this shrub is considered worthless or even a nuisance, but it was a valuable part of the Paiute economy, and the skill of the natives in using the bark attracted the attention of Peter Skene Ogden, who called it "wormwood." On Monday, July 9, 1827, he wrote in his Journal: "I observe for two miles beyond their Camp they had peel'd the bark of the wormwood. It is with this they manufacture their "scoop" nets, their lines and ropes for their horses, and it answers well almost equal to those manufactured with hemp."

Sagebrush was, and still is, a source of quick and intense heat when used for firewood. Those who have had the privilege of cooking or camping within smell of a sagebrush fire can appre-

Fig. 55. A side view of atlatl weights shows the flat side common to all.

Fig. 56. A back view reveals the rounded shape and groove for the cord.

Fig. 57.
Raven nest.

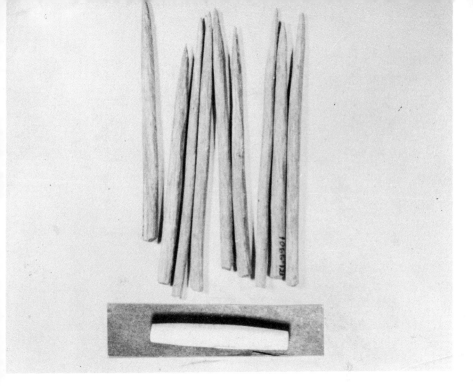

Fig. 58. Stick "counters" and bone. (From the Odell Collection in the Klamath County Museum)

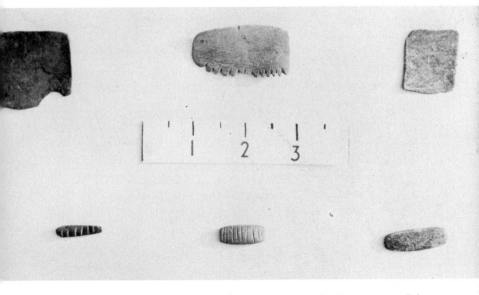

Fig 59. Thin bone pieces that collectors call money are shown in the upper row. Below are bone dice for the "woman's game."

ciate one of the few rewards of the Paiute's life. It was a hard life
that offered no security and little pleasure. The Paiutes had to
compete with rabbits for the plants of the desert, and with coyotes for such animal food as the antelope, the rabbit, and the
mule deer. Rabbit was not considered a liability, however. The
long net used in rabbit drives was undoubtedly an effective
method of stocking the table and supplying skins for the woven
rabbit blankets so valuable during the cold, dry winters.

Gambling among the Indians

One great pleasure that the Paiute—like all other Indians—
enjoyed was gambling. Bernard DeVoto called the midwest
Indians the "drunkards of gambling." The sticks and bones of
Fig. 58 are components of the "stick game," a favorite of the
Klamaths as well as many other tribes. It involved the hiding of
a polished bone in one hand or the other, with the opponent challenged to guess which hand held the bone. Stick counters were
passed from the losing side to the winners until all the sticks
were on one side. The stakes were then passed to the winner and
a new game began. Since many persons might place wagers in
the game, the players who possessed the most "power" were cho-
sen to represent the group. Chanting and invoking the gods was
permissible for all. A blind person would occasionally manipulate
and hide the bone because of his ability to maintain a "poker
face" in times of stress.

In Indian society, gambling was often accompanied by complex rituals. The legends of the Calapooia Indians recall elabo-
rate preparations of a spiritual nature, including bathing and
prayer, prior to participation in a gambling session. Early ob-
servers of these affairs reported that on occasion the Indian's
entire worldly goods might be staked in a contest — including
wives and members of the family. Losses were accepted without
complaint or self-pity.

Sometimes whole villages would take sides in a stick game,
which could last for several days. Gaming was also carried on in

a smaller scale between individuals. The lower part of Fig. 59 shows three bone dice thought to be used in such a game. The purpose of the thin bone pieces in the upper part of the picture is unknown, but they were called "money" by amateur collectors. They could also have been used as counters for a game.

The dice or casting bones in Fig. 60 are woodchuck teeth (marmot) which have been carved with varying marks. These pieces were used in the "woman's game." The combination of the marked or unmarked side that turned up after the dice were cast determined the winner.

Another combination of primitive artifacts thought to be a game was found by Leroy Gienger of Chiloquin, Oregon. Fig. 61 shows these stone balls which were uncovered by the desert wind on one of the ridges in Christmas Lake Valley. There were fifteen balls in the group when they were found, and they were arranged in a cluster around the largest ball. The size of the graduated smooth stones is from one and a half to about ten inches in diameter.

A group of five similar stones from Warner Valley appears in Fig. 62, row 2. These are neither so carefully fashioned nor graduated in size like the ones in the Gienger collection. One ball is flatter than the others, yet their grouping suggests that they had been used together. The balls in row 1 were found in a Modoc village on Lower Klamath Lake but were not associated when found. Row 3 consists of balls picked up at various sites in the Klamath highland and in the desert to the east.

An Indian gave this explanation of the stone balls: "They are bowled toward a hole in the earth. The object of the game is to see if your medicine is stronger than your competitor's and you can make the ball stay out of the hole when your opponent is bowling."

Legends and interviews with old-timers support the fact that there was no moral stigma involved in Indian gambling, and the help of the gods was vocally and emotionally called forth. He

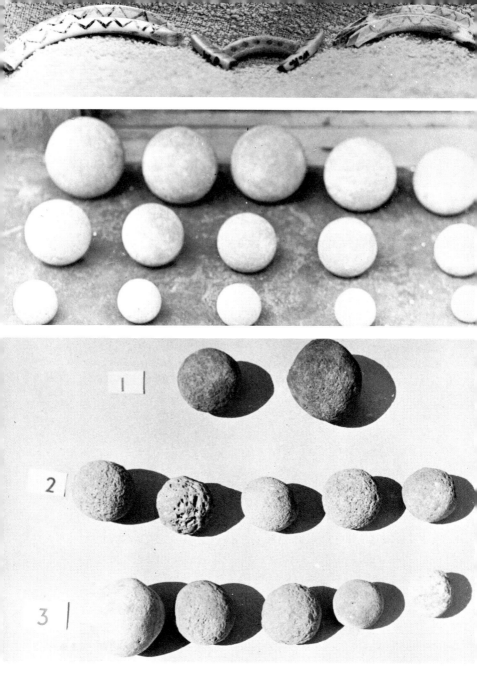

Fig. 60. (top) Marked woodchuck teeth also served as dice.

Fig. 61. (center) Components of a stone-age ball game.

Fig. 62. (bottom) Natives used stone balls for various purposes.

who had the power or luck was the one for whom the gods had intended it. Luck didn't just happen.

Lakeview Was Built in Snake Country

From the Pit River country in Northeastern California, a high ridge of mountains, the Warner Range, extends north across the Oregon border and along the east side of Goose Lake. The lofty peaks of the Warners capture from the westerly winds such moisture as may have passed over the Cascades. Creeks feed down from both slopes of this range as the winter snows gradually melt in the spring. The Pit River derives part of its water from this source, and a portion goes into Goose Lake.

Goose Lake, like Silver Lake, fluctuated greatly with the wet and dry weather cycles. Lakeview, claimed by the residents to be "Oregon's tallest town," was not far from the edge of Goose Lake at the time the town was founded. When the damming of Drew's Creek for irrigation caused the waters of the lake to recede, the wagon tracks of the pioneers were found far to the south of Lakeview. The location of the tracks proved that there had been a previous dry weather cycle within the time of the establishment of the Southern Route.

North from Lakeview the country rises gently along the slopes of the Warners, then descends again into the Abert Lake Basin. Abert Lake, which lies under magnificent Abert Rim, receives such water as may be left in the Chewaucan River but has never had an outlet to the sea. Accumulated chemicals have given it the characteristics of the shores of the Great Salt Lake and other bodies of water whose only outlet is evaporation by the sun. Many Indian artifacts have been found in the vicinity of Abert Lake by those who were willing to carry on a dispute with a rattlesnake over the right of way.

The territory around Oregon's tall town of Lakeview was occupied by the Snakes in historic times. The frontier between the Modocs and Snakes would have been west of Goose Lake, but there was no established line since both were semi-nomadic.

One of the nation's great earth faults is on the east side of Abert Lake in Lake County. Paiute paintings can still be seen on rocks along the shore.

Large, broken boulders mark the end of the long flow of obsidian at Glass Mountain, California.

There seems to be evidence that at times the Snakes ranged as far west as Beatty in Klamath County.

The Snakes were Hard to Dislodge

Centuries of living off the land made the Snake Indians troublesome for the settlers, and when the new Klamath Indian Reservation was established by the Treaty of 1864, many Snakes were rounded up and settled on the reservation. Apparently they had little taste for this more bountiful mode of life and the togetherness with their traditional enemies, the Klamaths, for they deserted the reservation to return to their sage and rimrock refuge in Warner Valley. Dave Hill, a Klamath chief, was an interpreter at the reservation and was persuaded, along with other Klamaths and some Modocs, to join in the chase for the fugitive Snakes. He told his story of the combined soldier and Indian expedition into the faulted mountains of Lake County to Albert Gatschet. Gatschet recorded it in both the Klamath and English language for the Smithsonian Institution. Here is a part of Chief Hill's story in his own words:

"Then we a lake went around and us noticed the Snakes; the dust they perceived; then Warner Ridge we climbed. Some through the lake waded; that was named Warner. Then at Camp Warner we day and night camped. . . . down antelope's trail we looked. . . . Then at nightfall made a fire the Snakes. There in the cliffs below there was a cave. Very cold that time—the wind blew and in the night the Snakes came and fired and the soldiers took fright and we got ready and we marched the same night. Southwards we went. The whole night we marched far away on the mountains. Then we stopped there in the early hours. They enslaved that time seven women; brought we those; then we again encamped from Goose Lake north side of a little west. . . and a Brook there is running [probably Drew's Creek] and at night came the Snakes—and not we slept all night, not we slept."

The Snakes were evidently determined to recover the seven women even at the risk of death or capture. It is easy to understand why the army party did not sleep well under this circumstance. Hill related that the enemy again returned in the morning, but the soldiers missed them with their rifles "by a long way." After pursuing them on horseback, the army lost all track, then gave up the chase. The Modoc and Klamath warriors were rewarded with a gift of two horses and five Snake women which they brought back to Fort Klamath. The army party separated from the rest and returned to Surprise Valley. In Dave Hill's time, the motives and rewards of warfare had changed but little from many generations before him. He mentioned of the lieutenant in charge, "Two Snake females he took with him." He did not say if the officer selected the two who were the best cooks.

One of the most unusual places in the western United States lies just east of the Warner Mountains on the Oregon side of the state line, Warner Valley. There are several reasons for this: its geological structure, its wildlife, its archeological features, and its beauty. The valley is dominated by magnificent Hart Mountain, which is much higher than it appears from the floor of Warner Valley. The floor itself is over four thousand feet in altitude and the mountain is such a tremendous block of stone that its mass is accentuated by the shape rather than the height. Any member of "The Order of the Antelope"—a conservation group that camps there annually—can tell you that the mountain is high, well over eight thousand feet.

Lakes and Caves of Warner Valley

If you look south from the top of Hart Mountain, the clear desert air permits a view of northern California and Nevada. Northward, the gigantic fault in the earth stretches toward Burns in Harney County. On the western side, the Rabbit Hills and Coyote Hills lie between Warner Valley and another great fault, Abert Rim, which overlooks the eastern shore of Abert Lake. The most thrilling view from the edge of Hart Mountain is directly below to the valley floor. Here lies a string of lakes ranging from the south at the California line. These include: Crump, Hart, Campbell, Anderson, Stone Corral, and Blue Joint Lakes.

The lake basins are separated from each other by low ridges of light tan soil that seems to have blown from the lake beds.

During a series of dry years, the lakes are only dry, flat basins cracked into hexagonal forms and marked by white rims around the edges where the alkali accumulates. During these arid cycles the shoreline, rising away from the prevailing winds, builds up higher as the sagebrush and rabbit brush catch the wind-borne soil in the eddies. Back from the immediate shore lie the older ridges, which are being eroded rather than built up.

During wet cycles the water level rises in the lakes and as it gets higher it breaks through the sand from one lake into another, washing channels which connect the lakes like a crooked string of beads. Far across the valley toward the west is the little village of Plush, and farther south, Adel. Both settlements were established on creeks; Plush on Honey Creek, and Adel on Deep Creek. Above each of these towns the creeks cut through more than a hundred feet of alluvial soil deposit before reaching the valley floor. Deposits indicate that the whole valley was a great lake during post-glacial times, forming a neck of Lake Bonneville. The lake has cut caves in the side of Hart Mountain and Poker Jim Ridge and has left a distinct shoreline nearly two hundred feet above the present valley floor. The rocks are stained with the alkalis of the centuries, having formed when the great lake, with no outlet to the sea, gradually evaporated.

The valley now has abundant wildlife. The playa lakes are full and in the proper season populated with ducks, geese, cranes, and the smaller wading birds. The presence of pelicans indicates that fish are also there. Antelope and deer, abundant in the refuge above on Hart Mountain, can often be seen in competition with the old friend of the Indian, the rabbit. The cliffs of Hart Mountain have been stocked with bighorn sheep with marked success.

A Snake with Fangs

Many adventurers who would welcome a chance for a mountain climb or a trip through the forest would reject an invitation for a long walk across a lonely desert in search of Indian camps. I suspect that arrowhead hunters and prospectors have something in common—a yearning for the unknown or the undiscovered which sends them on quests into uncomfortable and hazardous areas.

The desert has a strong appeal but it also has its drawbacks, the most dangerous being the ticks which can carry the deadly spotted fever. Rattlesnakes are sometimes found in the vicinity of Abert Lake, Summer Lake, and Warner Valley, though nearly all that I have seen have merely slid away into the rocks or brush on my approach. A few have coiled but none have come toward me.

Despite my assurances of the safety of being in the company of ticks and rattlesnakes, my wife has small enthusiasm for joining me in my long walks across the Warner Valley Desert. On one occasion I was able to persuade a friend, Roy ("Doc") Cook, to join me for a campout on the desert.

Doc was a man of ample girth who maintained a neatly trimmed, waxed mustache. This sharp-pointed facial adornment gave him a distinctly individual, and somewhat dapper appearance. He was also distinguished by his ability to take bird and nature pictures of a professional quality. A pharmacist by profession, Doc was well known in the Klamath area as a philosopher and traveler. At the time I invited him to accompany me to Warner Valley, I did not regard him as a rugged type but as an interesting companion.

The 22-automatic pistol which Doc carried I considered as more of an adornment than a protective device because it would only serve to anger a range bull. The strike of a rattlesnake, if it were to come, would be so quick that the gun would be too late to be effective.

We had not advanced more than a mile into the soft dunes of the valley floor when the sharp report of Doc's pistol came from the tall greasewood on the high dune above me. Puffing from the exertion, I arrived at the top of the dune to see him staring into the eyes of a coiled rattlesnake, its tail buzzing with indignation. "I missed him," Doc said, "but I'm not going to waste any more shells on him."

I had no idea why Doc had decided not to shoot any more. He may have been sore because he missed the buzzing target, but he just glowered back at the diamondback. Rattlesnakes have an evil look about them that nonpoisonous snakes do not seem to have. I suspect that a person who has never seen a rattler would recognize one by the head even if the tail were out of sight.

Pulling off a branch of a nearby sagebrush, Doc waved it in front of the coiled snake. The rattler struck like a coiled spring, extending his full length upon the sandy earth. My companion jumped upon the back of the extended serpent and trampled the twisting form into the dust. When I was able to overcome my astonishment I said, "Doc, you scared me to death!" He remarked casually that snakes can't strike for any distance unless they have a chance to coil.

After this incident I looked with new respect upon my mustachioed friend. I have since killed several rattlers but have never had the inclination to use Doc Cook's technique.

Artists in Stone

The small triangular Shoshonean-type arrowhead is found around the springs and lakes on the top of Hart Mountain where the Snakes stalked antelope. Evidence of their presence is also found on the shores of the ridges which separate the playa lakes of the valley below. The forces of erosion have uncovered here a type of projectile point which is quite different. Most are larger, more beautifully made, and in a wider variety of materials. The points are definitely not the later Shoshonean type and many are unusual in shape and workmanship.

The Columbia River and Calapooia points have become famous for the beauty of their shape and material. Those of Warner Valley deserve first rank for their quality of workmanship. Those workmen were the true Michelangelos of the stone chipper's or knapper's art. Fig 63, from the collection of Gene Favell of Klamath Falls, shows some of this beautiful chipping. Mr. Favell, a native of Lake County, has accumulated a collection of projectile points of such exquisite beauty that each item deserves to be classified as art. Many other collections also have been enriched from the thousands of artifacts found in the bed of Crump Lake. In Lakeview, Oregon, the Indian Village Restaurant has become a major tourist attraction as a result of the display of artifacts found in that region.

During dry weather cycles the flow of waters in Deep Creek and Honey Creek is greatly reduced. Much of the remaining water was used for irrigation. These factors, plus the evaporation in the air, dried up a large portion of Crump Lake. Sand-blasting winds soon tore away the black muck which coated the lake bottom. As the muck was removed, literally thousands of projectile points, knives, and drills were found, some in the black soil, and some in the yellow sand beneath it. Even considering the accumulation of the centuries, the numbers and types of artifacts exposed is hard to explain.

Blades, a Medium of Exchange

There is no doubt that the Indians cached quantities of chipped objects, sometimes finished, sometimes blanks. One cache of forty-nine knives was reported found at Silver Lake. I have seen caches of four knives and of five. The great distance which a number of the stones have been carried establishes chipped stone objects as an important item of aborigine trade.

David Cole, head of the Department of Oregon Archeology at the University of Oregon, has spent much time studying the habits of Oregon's prehistoric people. He explains the great number of chipped pieces found by saying that the large and unusual pieces were also prestige status symbols—the Lincolns and Cadillacs of the stone-age set. Such an explanation seems logical for the manufacture of many of the pieces in Warner Valley. There would be no utilitarian reason for producing pieces of such deli-

Fig. 63. Delicacy of design and workmanship.

Fig. 64. Crump Lake types.

cacy and shape as those in Fig. 64. The chipping was done by specialists in the tribe. One or two such workmen might finish arrowpoints for an entire village. In many cases the workmanship of individuals, sometimes poor, sometimes good, can be recognized; it is as though they had included a trademark on their product. The individuality of the artisan can be detected in Fig. 65.

Fig. 66 shows three blades. The top piece is a Warner Valley product ten inches in length. The Rogue River Valley Shasta knife is 15½ inches long and was found near Ashland, Oregon. Prestige pieces of this type were more common among the Shastas than on the east side of the Cascades. The small knife of yellow jasper is from Crump Lake in Warner Valley. In an article in *The American Anthropologist*, Vol. 7, No. 4, H. M. Rust tells of a canoe trip among the Shastas on the Klamath River, at the time they were still using the blades for their ceremonies and dances. Rust wrote:

"During a canoe voyage on the Klamath and Trinity rivers in Northern California in 1898, the author had occasion to visit many Indian villages, and to take the opportunity to make special inquiry for obsidian spears, knives, or swords, as they are commonly called. Ten in all were seen and five procured. They measured in length from seven to fifteen inches and two to four inches in width, and are beautifully chipped to the edge from end to end. In color the obsidian is black, red, or gray.

"In almost every instance, the owners were reluctant to show these blades. All were carefully wrapped in redwood bark and carefully hidden away, sometimes under the floor of the lodge but oftener outside beyond the knowledge of anyone except the owner. In one instance the owner could not be induced to get his blade until nightfall in order that no one should learn of its hiding place. This habit of secreting valuable articles for safety no doubt accounts for such objects having been found at times in isolated places remote from dwellings or burial places."

The experience of Rust helps confirm the theory of David

Fig. 65. Massive point contrasts with delicate ones from Crump Lake.

Fig. 66. The yellow jasper Crump Lake knife is dwarfed by the long Shasta knife from Ashland, Oregon, and the 10-inch Warner Valley blade at the top.

Cole that the obsidian objects were made for purposes of wealth as well as for utility. Both caches that were discovered when I was among those present were marked for future recovery by the person who had hidden the particular cache. On one cache the mark was a knife placed upright in the soil. In another case the cache was marked by a flat stone. Fig. 67 shows that cache found by Audrey McPherson near Table Mountain.

A Goose-Lake knife, twenty-two inches in length, is pictured in Warren K. Morehead's *Stone Age in North America*. The longest knife I have seen from this area is the one found by Jim DeVore; this is 13½ inches long. There are several knife fragments from Modoc cremations now in the Klamath County Museum. They were probably "dance rocks" or ceremonial blades brought out by their owners only for special occasions. Judging by the width and shape of the pieces, the original knives probably exceeded fifteen inches in length before they were broken and cast into the funeral pyre. Enough fragments of large Shasta-type ceremonial blades have been found to prove the existence of the trade pattern with the Modoc people.

Wide Variety of Arrows Used

The collector who has achieved a degree of sophistication in his hobby sometimes turns from numbers to beauty of craftsmanship and then to variety. Fig. 68 shows a number of odd-shaped pieces. Those in the bottom row are from Warner Valley, where the variety of forms equals that of any area of Indian habitation. Others in the figure are from Lower Klamath Lake. It is only natural that people who made and used so many projectile points should also need the smoothers to prepare the wooden shafts for the arrows, darts, and spears. Warner Valley has been the source of most of those shown in Fig. 69. There they selected a light sandstone that seems to be infused with bits of pumice, which gives it an excellent cutting quality. The arrow smoothers from other sites in the Klamath highlands were usually made from volcanic scoria stone with a good cutting edge. The various types

Fig. 67. This cache of fine blades was marked by a smooth, flat stone.

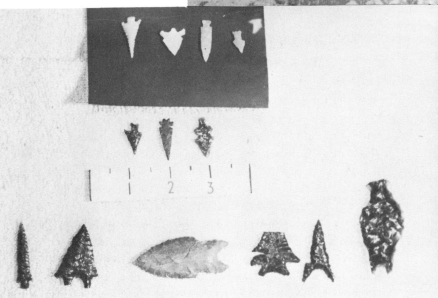

Fig. 68. Some stone age artists liked to be different.

Fig. 69. Arrow-shaft smoothers were made from coarse stones.

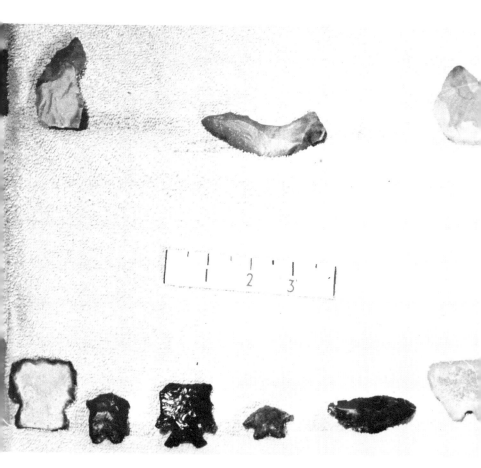

Fig. 70. Some scrapers were fitted for the attachment of a handle.

of grooving shown in the picture indicates the rubbing technique
of the arrow maker.

Scrapers and Drills

Among the specimens least prized by collectors are the
chipped objects known as scrapers, such as those shown in Fig.
70. From the standpoint of utility, these pieces were probably
used more often—and were more useful—than other chipped tools.
The apparent desire to secure unusual material may indicate that
the scrapers were designed for jobs which the more plentiful obsidian would not serve. The scrapers in the bottom row of the
figure have been constructed so that a handle or shaft could be
attached. Fig. 71 shows that some from the Silver Lake region
are very similar to those of Warner Valley except that fewer were
provided with a point of attachment for a handle. Many scrapers
took no special form but were simply pieces of stone or obsidian
that happened to be available when needed.

Scrapers were employed for various purposes such as shaping
bone objects, removing sinew from the muscle and bone of an
animal, and shaping and smoothing bows and arrows. The aborigines who lived under Hart Mountain Rim, either the Snakes
or the post-glacial people, left great numbers of mussel shells in
their camping places. Some of the so-called scrapers would have
been a handy tool for opening these shells.

Among the most beautiful and sought-after of the chipped
objects are drills (Fig. 72). Those in row 1 are from the Silver
Lake-Fort Rock region; those in row 2 are from the Lost River
Circle and Clear Lake area; those in row 3 are from Warner Valley, and the few in row 4 are from Lower Klamath Lake.

It seems strange that so few drills have been found at Lower
Klamath Lake since the total number of chipped objects in the
collection of the writer is greater from that area. The type and
quality is also inferior to those from the east. Another feature
that sets the drills apart from other chipped artifacts is the type
of stone used for their manufacture. A much higher proportion

Fig. 71. A wide variety of material and shapes was used for scrapers.

were made from colored stone than from obsidian. An oddity about the drills is that they seldom show signs of wear or abrasion. It suggests that they may have had other purposes, such as for pins or hair ornaments.

Four general types of drills are found, and these types are not hard to distinguish (Fig. 73). One type is designed to be turned in the hand like a skate key and used without attachment. A second type is fitted for attachment to a shaft similar to the way a projectile point would be attached. Such shafts were rolled between the hands or used with a bow much like a fire-by-friction apparatus. A third type of drill is nearly round in diameter and pointed at both ends. This type appears to have been mounted by being imbedded into the end of a wooden drill shaft.

In Fig. 73, a fourth type is shown on the right of No. 4. This simply consists of a fractured point of obsidian, shaped only by the fracture, with no sign of flaking except at the point of use. It seems likely that this type could also have been used as pins or buttons. Frank Payne found a number of such flakes in association with a cremated skeleton.

A fifth type of drill, called a microdrill, is reported as being abundant in an excavation of a Chumash Village near Santa Barbara, California. William Harrison, of the University of California at Los Angeles, has carefully sub-classified these according to length and diameter of bit, in addition to the shape of the stem. Such microdrills were used extensively by the Calapooia Indians of the Willamette Valley, but seem not to have been used extensively in Warner Valley or the Klamath Highland.

An Artist beneath Hart Mountain

An unusual drill was discovered by an unusual person in Warner Valley in 1937. The drill was made of a shiny white stone and was about seven inches long, with points on either end and a circular portion in the center for a handle. The unusual person was the artist, William McDermitt of Los Angeles. Long an art teacher at Washington State College, McDermitt quit teaching in

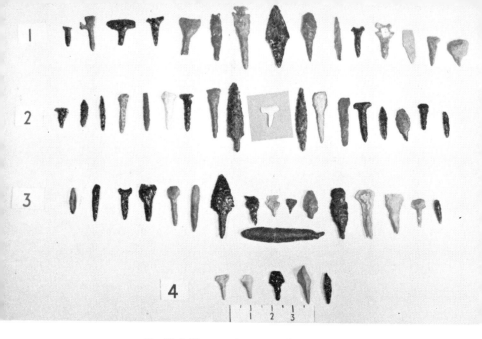

Fig. 72. Drills were often made of colored stone.

Fig. 73. (below) Some drills were fashioned for mounting on a shaft, others for use with the fingers.

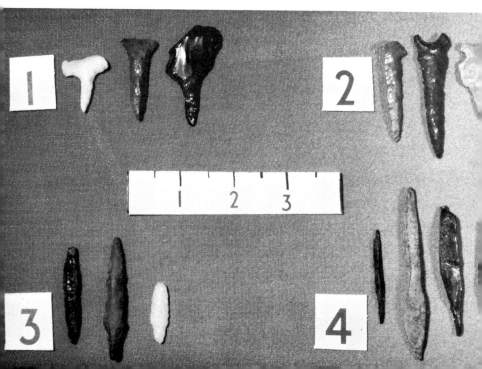

order to paint. His visits to the valley were made in a model-A Ford. A black umbrella provided him protection from the sun and a weapon for use against rattlesnakes. His great delight was to sketch with water color the dynamic quality of the purple, black, and gold storm clouds which roll out toward Hart Mountain from the Rabbit and Coyote hills. He would sit in the wind on his portable chair, without fear of the lightning flashes—and delight in capturing on canvas the mood and feeling of the great valley.

Warner Valley

The desert in north Warner Valley is quite different from the Fort Rock Desert. Actually, deserts are almost as variable from each other as lakes. The Mohave of California differs greatly from the Chihuahua country of Mexico. The domain of the old Mimbres people in southern New Mexico varies considerably from that of their contemporaries, the Hohokams of southern Arizona.

One way in which the Warner country differs from the Fort Rock area is that the thorny greasewood is more abundant in Warner Valley than the sagebrush and rabbitbrush, both of which dominate the plant growth around Fort Rock and Christmas Valley. Another striking feature of the Warner country is the way in which the dry air sucks the moisture from the human body and brings on thirst. It may be that the long vertical rock which forms the side of Hart Mountain and Poker Jim Ridge has a tendency to dry the air. This giant fault faces in the right direction to absorb much of the heat generated by the afternoon sun. This hot wall, combined with the hot and thirsty soil, creates a humid condition sharply affecting the person who travels the valley floor; such a traveler will undergo more rapid dehydration than in any other place I have seen. During the summer, residents of the valley ventured across the great dunes only on horseback.

Dangerous Duck Soup

One incident stands out in my experiences which illustrates the problems of thirst in this desert country. My brother Harry is a native webfoot of the Willamette Valley, where he once conducted a mortuary in Lebanon, Oregon. On one occasion, in June during the thirties, he accompanied me into Warner Valley; this was his first try for the beautiful "owl-eared" arrowpoints. I told him of the dehydration problem and said that I would not eat any breakfast and would eat little or no lunch during the hot, dry trek across the valley floor. Being a creature of habit, he had his usual bacon for breakfast and carried a couple of sandwiches along with his canteen of water.

The only travel on the soft valley floor is by walking or by horseback. This seems torturously slow to the arrow hunter, eager for the rich bonanza he visualizes on the distant dunes. The high humps of earth require a considerable amount of uphill work while the soft fluffy nature of the soil causes sinking and sliding. Progress of the hunter is further slowed when the channels which connect the lake contain water. He must remove his clothing and carry it in a bundle overhead as he proceeds to sink his bare toes deep into the soft mud with each step. When the depth approaches arm-pit level and the bottom of the coffee-colored channel ahead is still unknown, the sensible person has cause to reflect upon the ridiculous position into which he has voluntarily maneuvered himself.

On this particular occasion, I recall that Harry carried his pocket watch in his mouth when he waded the channels—an added precaution in case the depth required him to swim. At noon he ate his sandwiches, and we then changed course, swinging back toward our point of departure. We had marked the place where our car could be found by observing the notches in the rocks of the great escarpment. The return trip is always faster, even though it is hotter and you are more tired. Gradually I began to feel some effect of dehydration. Although Harry did not complain, I noticed that his lips were quite dry and beginning to crack.

Even though the arrow hunting was fairly good, I had a sense of urgency to get back to the east side of the valley and to our water can. As the sun burned the air into shimmering heat waves, hunting Indian artifacts became of secondary importance; getting back came first. We moved along faster, not stopping to rest or examine the soil. Rabbits darting from the brush or locusts imitating the sound of rattlesnakes ceased to startle us as they had on the trip out. As my mouth became drier, I placed a small pebble in it in an effort to relieve the dryness. At first it seemed to help, but soon it served no useful purpose. I knew that Harry must be in even worse shape than I.

At last we came in view of the channel that we had waded. Harry's pace quickened and I matched it out of the desire to stay close. Without wasting words, he knelt and spread his handkerchief on the warm channel water near the muddy shore. Then, lying with his chest in the mud, he sucked the liquid through the handkerchief until he had enough. I was torn between my desire for water and my fear of what I knew it must contain.

My dry paunch cried out for water, but hours spent over a microscope caused the cerebrum to win the decision. I could see daphnids, cyclops, and other twisting creatures in that water. My awareness of the minute size of invisible beasties that would filter through the cloth restrained me from joining my brother in his prone position and utter enjoyment. We then hurried on to the car to replace our lost body fluids from a cream can of warm water (without bugs).

I was sure that all sorts of parasites would attack the insides of my impetuous companion but he was even stronger the next day, and he suffered no later ill effects. I doubt that the warm, duck-flavored water even served to break his habit of eating salty bacon before taking a long hike.

This marsh scene of an Indian dugout shows the ideal Klamath environment—food, protection, and easy transportation. (From Maude Baldwin Collection in Klamath County Museum)

4. THE WOCAS PEOPLE

Habitat of the Klamaths

To understand the Navajos, one must understand the desert; to understand the Klamaths, one must know about the marsh. The marsh provided all things to the Klamaths — their shelter, their food, and many of their legends. In more than 7,500 years of living near the marsh, the Klamaths made such a complete and successful adaptation to their surroundings that they developed a culture as unique to their area as the culture of the Navajos was to their dry and sunny Southwest.

The Klamaths called themselves the Lake People, but it was from the periphery of the lakes and the adjacent streams, springs, and marshes that they obtained the things which made possible the sustenance and development of their tribe. To those unfamiliar with it, marsh habitat seems a strange place. A description of it is a necessary part of any explanation of either the social patterns or material culture of the Klamaths.

The mouth of the Williamson River was one of the most populous centers of Indian habitation from ancient times until well into the historic period. The river channels have changed over the centuries, but the people have lived there for so long that even the old meander channels show signs of ancient occupants.

A description of the setting at the mouth of the Williamson could apply to many places where the springs and streams enter the lake. This river draws much of its waters from the Klamath Marsh to the north. It is joined by the Sprague River at Chiloquin, which derives considerable water from the Sycan Marsh in Lake County. From this genesis, both streams carry a heavy burden of nutrients, both organic and chemical. This fertility results in a virtual explosion of plant and animal growth in Klamath Lake. The water so teems with life that the marsh covers itself rather than erodes.

Travel in the Marsh Country

There is no such thing as a good way to travel in such a place. A step causes the earth to shudder; bubbles appear and gases arise. The traveler does not know if he will sink to his ankles or to his armpits—it is too thick to swim in, too thin to walk upon.

Officials of the Fish and Wildlife Service have a small flat-bottomed boat driven by an airplane propeller which enables them to get around in comparatively shallow water, but even this craft is helpless where the heavy growth of tules impedes progress. The Klamath Indians helped to overcome the problem of moving about on the soft bottom of the marsh by the invention of the marsh shoe, a drawing of which appears in Fig. 74; this is copied from one by O. T. Mason in the Smithsonian Report of 1902. The original specimen is catalog No. 24109, now in the National Museum.

The dugout canoe was the most common method of conveyance for open-water use in fishing, or for movement in deeper water among the leaves of the wocas plant. Paddles were useless in the thick leaves or in the shallower water. So a pole, with the split end held apart by a small stick or bone, became the accepted means of propulsion. The Klamath canoe was slightly narrower at the prow end, and when paddles were used, the weight was placed toward the back. In poling the canoe, however, the occupant knelt in the prow in order to hold the boat on course and to be in a position to gather material from the water. Fig. 75 shows a Klamath canoe pole which is split at the lower end to keep it from sinking in the mud.

Four of the small dugouts used on the marsh for gathering wocas are shown in Fig. 76. They are smaller than the deep-water canoes. The lady pictured poling the watercraft is evidently posing rather than gathering wocas.

Both the Klamath Marsh canoe and deep-water boats had quite thin shells but were not ornamented like those of the northwest coastal Indians. Samuel Clark, the New York *Times* reporter, observed that earth was sometimes carried in one end of the boat to enable the user to build a fire for cooking. A small, cheery fire can be appreciated almost anywhere, but in the vastness of the marsh it would have been especially valued. Here, the feeling of isolation is increased by the dense growth of large tules and cattails which obscure vision. Below the surface, the dark water bears a heavy burden of organic stain, plus both plant and animal life—some floating on the water, some in it. This opaque liquid makes it impossible to tell what is in the water or just under the surface.

A Wildlife Paradise

Algae and free-floating plants create a paradise for ducks, geese, and wading birds. Strange bugs and crustaceans, ranging from the tiny transparent daphnids to the many varieties of swimming larvae, provide abundant food for the turtles and frogs. Cranes, herons, and beautiful white egrets also work the shore during the proper season of their migration.

While the marsh is a lonely place for the uninitiated—in the right season, at the right time of day, it becomes a scene of great activity. Toward evening the weird cry of the loon seems to be a signal for a series of events. First, the water is rippled as a female muskrat swims past carrying the tules for her winter house. This house of reeds will in turn form a platform for the nest of the Canadian Goose in the spring. If the season is late spring, a

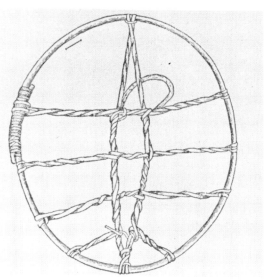

Fig. 74. Mud shoes similar to snow shoes enabled the Klamaths to travel in the marsh. (Sketch by O. T. Mason in Annual Smithsonian Report of 1902)

Fig. 75. Split end of the canoe pole kept it from sinking in the mud. A small stick held the end apart.

Fig. 76. (below) Small marsh canoes in a wocas patch. (Smithsonian Report, 1902)

mother grebe may glide by—undulating her long neck as her saucy chick rides on her back.

In summer, the warm afternoon brings to maturity the pupae of the many gauzy-winged insects. They rise almost in clouds as they emerge from the water. It is then that the tern and swallow offer their demonstration of aerial acrobatics, feeding on the wing and almost in rhythm to the sounds emanating from the squawking, quacking, and croaking residents of the watery world beneath. From this watery world, the frog, otter, and crane entered the legends and healing arts of the Klamath people.

Snakes Kept Pressure on the Klamaths

It seems almost miraculous that the Klamaths were able to defend their homeland over the centuries from the more mobile and very aggressive Snake Indians. The Klamaths were good warriors, but the numerical odds greatly favored the Snakes. Not only the weight of numbers was against the marsh dwellers, but the life pattern of the wandering Shoshone groups called for them to be on the attack. Great social prestige and status was accorded the warriors or risk-takers in nearly all Indian cultures. The final result or profit from the risk was not so important as the dangers involved in the act itself. Among Plains Indians, the touching of an enemy gave great prestige; among the Snakes (Paiutes), who were neighbors of the Klamaths, the successful stealer of horses received great honor.

The modern-day athletic hero thus had his counterpart in Indian society, which honored the Indian who could harass the enemy, if not by killing, then by stealing his goods. Even Peter Skene Ogden, who was so often the victim of such prestige raids, came to have a certain admiration for the custom. On February 14, 1827, while he was traveling in the Umpqua country, he lamented the morals of the Indian residents in his Journal: "How far different and more generous and honourable are the Black Feet and the Snakes. They show considerable ingenuity and address in stealing horses and when pursued and overtaken they make all the resistance they can, but when in vain, resign themselves to their fate without expressing the least regret for their crime, but are surprised we do not retaliate in kind on theirs. With Indians in general, horse stealing is not considered a crime but viewed more as a profession, and with many tribes he that has been most successful in his different stealing excursions is generally selected and requested to take the lead when they start in numbers, and his plans and orders are strictly obeyed and promptly executed—all their hopes and confidence being placed, and seldom does he disappoint them. He however has arduous duty to perform and his life is more in danger than any other."

While Ogden understood—though he did not condone—the practice of raiding, it caused neighboring tribes to live in a state of continued anxiety.

In the long series of encounters with the Snakes, the marsh may have tilted the advantage toward the Klamaths and Modocs because of the natural barrier it created for conventional travel and the protective cover it provided. There was certainly no lack of effort on the part of the Snakes in carrying out forays into the territory of their neighbors.

In addition to the social value of raiding, a second characteristic of the Indian way of life was the ever-pressing occurrence of hunger. Hunger was not always the driving force in the case of the Umpquas or Shastas, but to the Snakes hunger seemed to be one of the accepted conditions of life. Famine or starvation was too often the motivating reason for the raiding parties.

The type of terrain occupied by the Snakes made a nomadic way of life a necessity. The good leader was one who could supply his people—whether from nature's products or from the storehouse of the enemy mattered little, as long as lean bellies could be filled and the young kept alive another season. Such pressures made Snake raids a continuing threat from the south bank of the Columbia throughout the entire area that they bordered. Lewis and Clark observed that Indians had been driven as far as the north shore of the Columbia by the Snakes.

The well-endowed lakes, marshes, and streams of the Klamath area would be natural places for the Snakes to give vent to their two great drives — prestige and hunger. Undoubtedly, for many generations, stories of Snake raids were repeated around the fires of the winter lodges of the Klamaths. It is easy to understand how they would look upon their marsh habitat, not as a smelly, treacherous barrier, but rather as a place of refuge and security, as well as food supply.

Klamath Indian Dwellings

The Klamath Marsh was also the scene for the first written record of the meeting of the white man with the Klamath Indian. The comfort and safety which their marsh home gave the residents is vividly recorded by Ogden, who made this entry in his Journal on November 29, 1826: "He [Thomas McKay—like Ogden, a brigade leader] found the Village composed of 20 tents and, strange as it may appear, built on the water and surrounded on all sides by water, and from its depth impossible to approach them on foot or on horseback—but with canoes with which they are well provided—their tents are well constructed for defense, being built of large logs in form and shape for block houses. The foundations of these tents are made with stone and gravel and made solid by piles sunk about six feet deep. Indeed the construction of their tents evinces great ingenuity. From their accounts they have many enemies to apprehend and are constantly guarded, and when they absent themselves from their village they remain in the mountains; and altho they express themselves well pleased to see us on their lands, still they could not but regret we had opened a communication.

" 'For many years past,' they informed us, 'the Nez Perce Indians have made different attempts to reach our Village but could not succeed, and even this last summer we discovered a war party of Cayuse and Nez Perce, who were in search of us but did not succeed, but now they will have in future your road, and altho we have no fire arms, still we fear them not—so far as

Fig. 77. The summer house could be moved easily and kept near the food supply. (From Maude Baldwin Collection in Klamath County Museum)

Fig. 78. Wocas blooms. This water lily was the corn of the Klamaths. (Van Landrum photo)

bows and arrows will assist, they are well provided—they have only one horse amongst them and the cause they assign for this is the winters are too severe and snow too deep.' "

Both the winter lodges and summer houses were located near the water whenever possible. There the Klamaths enjoyed not only the protection of the surrounding cover, but also the close source of food. In addition, the tules and cattails provided the material for mats used in their summer houses. The simple structure shown in Fig. 77 was stretched over bent willow and was well hidden in the surrounding growth. The metal pans beside the burden basket in the picture illustrate the change that was taking place in the lives of the Klamaths in the early 1900s.

Water Depth Determined the Food

As the depth of the water determined the biological zones, each zone made its distinctive contribution to the life of the Indians. Deep water provided fish and waterfowl. Less deep water was the habitat of the water lily, called wocas by the Indians. Still less deep and nearer the shore grew the tules, so useful for basketry, mats, and clothing. Fig. 78 shows the lily, which grows at a level between the open water and the tule so does not compete with it.

During the spring season, the lower end of the tule shoots were tender enough to serve for food. This tall reed in Klamath Lake sometimes extended growth out over the water; then, during storms, a segment would break away from the shore and become a floating island. Above the tule zone, in the moist, soft earth adjacent to the water grows the nettle plant. The unpleasant sting of the leaves of this plant was more than compensated for by the value of the fine, strong fiber from its bark. This silky filament made possible the thread and cordage so necessary to a fishing industry.

Food from Water-Lily Seed

The most distinctive feature in the life pattern of inhabitants of the Klamath Highland, and the one which made their culture unique, was the wocas industry. The seed of the great water lily (*Nymphaea polysepala*), together with fish, formed the main staples of their diet and challenged their inventive talent to create a complex harvesting process. A distinctive vocabulary, including several nouns, was even developed to describe the tools of manufacture and the stages through which the wocas was taken before it reached the edible phase.

When Frederick Vernon Coville, honorary curator of the Smithsonian Institution Division of Plants, was passing through the Klamath country in 1902, he became so intrigued by the wocas industry that he changed from botanist to ethnologist for an entire week to document this interesting process. He noted only two changes in their primitive implements as the result of the influence of white contact: first, a large iron frying pan was used in the parching process rather than the traditional mat (Fig. 79); second, the tow sack or gunny sack had replaced the storage basket. The adoption of the horse as a carrying animal undoubtedly made the use of the gunny sack possible.

The wocas plant grew upon many of the protected bays and river eddies in the Klamath country, but the greatest growing place was in the Klamath Marsh; there Coville reported ten thousand acres of wocas (Fig. 76). This became the mecca for Indian people during the month of the index finger. Prior to white contact, the Klamath people accounted for the months by naming them after the fingers on each hand; usually there was also a relationship with the gathering or harvesting of a certain crop. For example, the small finger month was for mullet; the thumb month for storing dried camas underground; and the wocas was gathered from mid-August into September.

Migrating from the river towns such as Chiloquin, they returned to their temporary camps on the great marsh to the north. The pine and fir canoes which had been preserved by being hidden under the dark waters of the marsh were brought forth, dried, and—upon the signal from the shaman—the harvest was begun. Little imagination is required to picture the excitement of the wocas season, when old friendships were renewed and old feuds continued. The influx of migrants was likely viewed with mixed emotions by the permanent residents of the marsh as they haggled the price of a slave or a gaming wager with the fishing people from the south.

The gathering of wocas was women's work. Men hunted antelope and deer, gambled, and brought wood to fire the green pods in the process of separating the seeds. Two kinds of seeds were gathered. The more mature seeds had separated from the disintegrating pod and floated freely in a gelatinous mass on the surface of the water. This mass was called "spokwas." It was scooped up in a split willow scoop, similar to that of Fig. 80, and placed in a basket in the canoe. These more matured seeds were valued more than the seeds gathered in the pods, but they consisted of only about ten percent of the harvest.

These seeds were processed by being placed in a fermenting vat or pit called a "spokwas hole." Coville wrote: "The pits are commonly 1½ to 2 feet in both diameter and depth. The top is covered with grass, tules, or an empty grain sack. These holes may be found anywhere about a wocas camp and from the inconspicuous character of their covering, among the miscellaneous furniture of an Indian's summer camp, it is altogether too easy to step into one. If a motto were to be suggested for visitors, it might well be: "Let the stranger in a wocas camp beware of the spokwas hole."

After a proper period of slow fermentation, the spokwas mixture—containing the seeds in a matrix of viscous liquid—was removed and placed again in the canoe. The canoe was then used as a vat, since water was added to the mixture. By rocking the canoe and kneading the contents, the Indian separated the seeds from the liquid; these rose to the top to be skimmed away.

The greatest part of the harvest consisted in picking the green pods containing the less mature seeds (Fig. 81). These pods were kept separate and thrown into other canoes. They were processed in a manner quite different from that of the free-floating mature

Fig. 79. The top mat was scorched from parching seeds.

Fig. 80. Willow scoops were used to pick up free-floating "Spokwas."

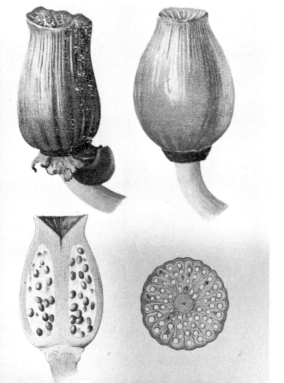

Fig. 81. Wocas seeds are encased in a soft green pod. (Annual Smithsonian Report, 1902)

seeds. The pods were fired in a mixture of pine limbs and needles until sufficiently cooked. The mass was then pounded on a dry surface with a stone maul (Fig. 82). Ashes or dry, rotten wood was added to the pods, causing the mixture to dry and separate from the seeds.

Coville does not mention the use of a wooden club in this stage of manufacture; however, a few clubs have been found upon some of the sites of the Klamath Marsh. No positive purpose for these great clubs has yet been suggested, but their size and weight is so great that they would be ineffective for hunting or combat. It seems likely, though, that their use must have been for separating the wocas seeds from the pods. Fig. 83 shows such a club donated to the Klamath County Museum by Leroy Gienger. He found six of these on one of the man-made islands of the Klamath Marsh. Scott Warren also found a similar club unearthed by a power shovel during a construction project.

Centuries of occupation were needed to build some of the islands at Klamath Marsh. It must have been on one such island —consisting largely of ashes and cooking rocks—that Ogden first encountered the Klamaths. The piling which he referred to was probably the support poles for the winter house.

Development of the Two-Horned Mano

Centuries of trial and error must have also been required to develop the tools necessary for the transition from a hunting to a wocas culture. The mano, a stone tool, provides an exceedingly interesting set of clues and steps illustrating this development. The flat, hand-sized stone was named from the Spanish word meaning hand. It is distributed throughout the western desert regions of the United States and was the principal tool used by the Pueblo peoples of the Southwest and by the Indians of Mexico, for grinding corn. The Indians of Oregon, of course, had no corn; but the mano—called a "grinder" by Coville—has been one of the commonest tools found as the processes of erosion have gradually uncovered the old camps.

Fig. 82. Plain mauls. The tops of some have been used as pestles.

Fig. 83. Giant club photographed in the Klamath County Museum.

Fig. 84. Many-sided manos, or hand-grinding stones.

Fig. 85. Manos were made in many different shapes and sizes.

Fig. 86. Thin manos.

Fig. 87. Three views of a mano that has been sharpened.

Fig. 88. These stones have been used for two purposes.

Besides being more numerous in the Klamath region than in any other area, the mano also appears in a wider variety of forms there than elsewhere. There are several reasons for this variation. The many different kinds of foods which made up the Indians' diet called for a variety of processing utensils. Dried fish and mussels, ipos, camas, wocas, and grass seeds were only a few of the foods which required grinding.

The many-faced manos in Fig. 84 seem to be found only at Clear Lake, but they occur there in considerable numbers. Possibly a specialized food was processed at this place, requiring such a surface as that of the mano. The one at the lower left in Fig. 85, a simple, rectangular, bi-faced stone, is the type most commonly found in Lake and Modoc counties, the domain of the Paiutes. The others in the figure give some idea of the difference in shapes. The small girdled mano in the center is most unusual and may have been used for an entirely different purpose.

The great variety in mano shapes at Clear Lake could have resulted from another reason. The same site could have been occupied by different tribes over a given number of centuries, with each tribe leaving the record of its occupation on the stones in the soil. The manos pictured in Fig. 86 were washed from the sands of Clear Lake. Nos. 1 and 2 are called "razor clam" shape. Nos. 3 and 4 are exceedingly thin. No. 4 seems to have been made of a volcanic bomb, and No. 5, a rare, round shape, is extremely porous.

Indian housewives frequently selected porous stones for making their grinding tools, especially their manos and mortars. This porous material provided a natural cutting surface to speed the milling of the food. On occasion they sharpened the grinding surface in order to do a better job. Fig. 87 gives three views of an unusually well-sculptured mano from the Bly area. The tool had been sharpened on the grinding surface (right) by etching grooves in it with another stone.

Manos were sometimes used for more than one purpose. In Fig. 88, the center mano and the one to the right have had pits ground into the upper surface as though for use as small mortars or as anvils. A more unusual dual use is the combination of net weight and mano shown at the left in Fig. 88.

The light, porous texture of some of the stones shaped like manos indicates that their principal use may have been for fleshing hides or rubbing and smoothing the surface of a canoe. The preparation of food with such a stone would likely leave a residue of grit and sand sufficient to make the food undesirable. One rectangular-shaped stone with abrasive qualities still serves the writer as an excellent tool to remove paint from a boat.

Another reason for the great variation of mano forms was the gradual development of the tool to improve its use in food processing. These variations took place over a long period of time and were made by many generations of people living in the same place. As the food habits of these prehistoric residents changed, the methods of preparing foods advanced. The evolution of the mano can be roughly compared to the changes which take place in car models over the years.

In arriving at the final form of the two-horned mano, several stages were involved. The first was probably a simple rock with one side, similar to the one at the far left in Fig. 89. This was improved by cutting a girdle around the edge of the stone to give the user a hand grip. Such girdled stones are fairly common in the homeland of the Klamaths, but are rarely found elsewhere. The third stage of development was a natural improvement of the girdled stone, providing a higher top or single ridge to allow for better manipulation. The second mano from the right in this picture is ridged, with a shallow groove cut across the top separating the two ends of the ridge into separate grips. This may represent a transition type. The stone at the far right has the two handles which are a trademark of the Klamath Tribe and the ultimate in the tools of the wocas culture.

The Klamath women have always — even in recent times — taken great pride in their manos; and the rhythm of their grinding task formed a basis for the songs which they sang to lighten

Fig. 89. Series illustrating possible developmental stages of the two-horned mano.

Fig. 90. Porous stone was usually favored.

Fig. 91. Single-horn grinders.

Fig. 92. Typical two-horned manos, the trademark of the Wocas People.

Fig. 93. The useless handles on these stones were probably made to stay in style.

the work of preparing wocas. This pride is certainly justifiable, for many centuries were required to bring about the changes from a simple pebble to the type that finally emerged.

A girdled stone and a modified, two-horned grinder are shown in Fig. 90. Both are scoriaceous lava, the favorite material. The group shown in Fig. 91 is of the single-horn or single-ridge type, believed by the writer to be a step in the transition toward the final tool. There is no doubt that both the single and two-horned manos were used concurrently. Both are found in the same strata of the old wocas culture sites on Upper Klamath Lake and the Klamath Marsh.

The five stones pictured in Fig. 92 are typical of the most usual shape. A rather strange social force is demonstrated by the ones shown in Fig. 93. The nibs or handles are much too low to have any value in manipulating the grinders. The only apparent reason for their manufacture was explained this way by a Klamath woman: "We are Klamath women. Klamath women use two-horned mealing stones; therefore, we shall put two horns upon these stones even though they have no utility." This "keeping up with the Joneses" should not seem strange to people who put six tail lights on their automobiles.

The ladies of Klamath Lake may have had a good reason for putting nibs on their grinding stones—but no one has yet suggested a plausible reason for the manufacture of the giant stone held by Leroy Gienger of Chiloquin in Fig. 94. If it were round it would be considered a pestle. If it were one sixth as long it could be a mano. Perfectly fashioned, it is not an unfinished object, yet its purpose defies explanation. The former Williamson River resident who made the long rectangular stone must have had considerable muscle, for great effort would be required to use it. He is perhaps chuckling in the Happy Hunting Ground over the puzzle he has left.

The fact that the two-horned mano is so distinctive to the Klamath region has provided an interesting type of clue for tracing Indian trade patterns and the dispersal of material culture.

Fig. 94. Too large for a grinding stone . . . what is it?

Fig. 95. Poor copies of manos made by neighboring people.

The first clue to the amazing distance of the prehistoric Indian trade was uncovered by J. A. Jeancon. His Smithsonian Institution report pictures a stone excavated in 1922 in the Chama Valley in New Mexico. It is described as a "Koshare Fetish," a type of medicine stone or ceremonial stone. This find by Jeancon is a perfect match for the round-based wocas grinders used on the Klamath Marsh. The Indian maiden who fashioned it was probably proud that she had provided a stone so beautiful and typical of the two-horned mano, the unique invention of her people. She could not forecast the great distance that it had to travel in order to be discovered in the New Mexico ruin.

An example of even greater distance for the barter between Indian tribes was provided by a find at Pecos, New Mexico. Here, A. V. Kidder, in his classic work on Southwest archeology, reported the discovery of a two-horned mano which competent anthropologists have identified as a Klamath wocas grinder. The find by Kidder is especially valuable for establishing an approximate date for the trade and in proving that the development of this tool had been completed by the year 1540. The year 1540 may now seem long ago, but to those whose ancestors were showered with the ash of Mount Mazama, it would be comparatively recent.

Naturally there has been some dispersal of the Klamath manos into the areas adjacent to their manufacture; however, N. G. Seaman reports in *Indian Relics of the Pacific Northwest* that none were found in his searches in the Fort Rock Desert region. The one mano of the two-horned variety pictured in his book is explained as typical of the Klamath Indians.

Other neighbors of the Klamaths evidently made efforts at manufacturing stone grinders with the two horns on the top, but there are detectable differences from those used by the inventors. Fig. 95 shows four manos from Clear Lake. These all have two nibs on the top, but they are longer and narrower in shape. It is not possible to tell whether the Indian women of Clear Lake, in trying to duplicate the Klamath tools, created a poor likeness, or if they purposely changed the design in order to adapt it to the grinding of a different food.

The vessel necessary to make use of the mano is the metate. Coville described its use in preparing wocas after watching the skillful women carry on the process. He calls the metate a "mealing stone" and writes as follows:

"The removal of the shells is accomplished by grinding the shells lightly on the ordinary grinding stone and winnowing them. The lower mealing stone (called lmach by the Klamaths) is a piece of flat lava rock commonly about a foot and a half in length and about ten inches in width. The upper stone (si-lak′-al-ish) is also lava and is much smaller. It usually has two nibs upon the back which fit into the hands of the user as she sits or kneels on the ground. The seeds to be ground are placed, a few handfuls at a time, on the end of the lower stone next to the grinder. The seeds on that side of the pile farthest from her are spread out in a thin layer reaching to or beyond the middle of the stone. She seizes the upper stone in both hands and rubs it lightly over the lower and over the thin layers of seed upon it.

"The forward stroke does the grinding, while the deft backward strike serves to catch between the stones a small amount of seeds from the thin edge of the lower pile on the lower stone. The product of the grinding accumulates on the edge of the lower stone farthest from the grinder and is shoved off upon a circular mat, or a very shallow, tightly woven dish, commonly called a wocas shaker, upon which the end of the mealing stone has been placed.

"The notable feature of the grinding of these seeds is that the shells are cracked so that they can be removed; while the kernels —from the tough, elastic texture they have acquired through their partial cooking and from the lightness of stroke exercised by the grinder—are not cracked as are the thoroughly dried or roasted seeds when similarly manipulated upon the mealing stone."

The numerous varieties in grades of wocas and the complicated stages in the preparation of the various grades show the

Fig. 96. A log raft today marks an old village site on Crystal Creek.

Fig. 97. Buck Island in Klamath Lake provided a fine refuge.

result of much trial-and-error experimentation by the Klamath women. Through centuries of industry and patience, they learned to derive the greatest value from the water-lily seeds. According to the maturity of the seeds alone, there were five grades of wocas: spokwas, stontablaks, lowak, nopapk, and chiniakum.

Upper Klamath Lake

The shore of Klamath Lake, Oregon's largest lake, is marked by many bays, peninsulas, and backwater marshes. The Cascade Mountains extend to the west shore. From that point eastward, there is an abrupt change in the vegetation, wildlife, and rainfall, as this line divides the Cascade region from the range and basin country toward the east. Mule deer range on one side of the lake, blacktail on the other. The human inhabitants seemed to show no pronounced preference for either side but made their villages according to the advantages offered by the terrain.

From the north and west a number of spring-fed streams bring clear, cool waters coursing into the darker waters of the marshes. Crystal Creek, shown in Fig. 96, is one example. Such streams provided a spawning place for fish. The protected water courses also made ideal campsites, for with a canoe the lake people could forage over a large area whether they were seeking duck eggs, trapping birds, or fishing.

Some of the principal fishing sites were at Crystal Creek, Harriman Lodge, Williamson River, Barclay Springs, Wood River, and Odessa Creek. All of the more prominent points of land were also occupied; among these are Eagle Ridge, The Skillet Handle, Squaw Point, and Coon Point. Where a peninsula exists, there is also a bay with its accompanying marsh. The shore of the lake is an almost continuous archeological site; however, the waters are now held back for purposes of irrigation and power. The result is that many of the village sites are under water most of the year.

There are two islands in Klamath Lake which were occupied by prehistoric Indians. The northern island, off Eagle Ridge, is called Bare Island. The southern island, near Cove Point, is still occupied by deer and is aptly called Buck Island (Fig. 97).

The gently sloping north end of Buck Island was heavily pop-ulated by Indians and shows signs of both fishing and wocas cul-ture. The east shore of the island was apparently a marsh at one time, as the peat beds show near the surface during periods of low water. The main reason for occupation of the island would seem to have been for protection; otherwise the inconvenience of reach-ing shore over an often rough and sometimes impassable lake would hardly have made the island a desirable homesite.

Next in size to the Williamson River village was Eulalona, on the south end of Klamath Lake, where Link River leaves the lake. Eulalona extended on both sides of Link River for over a half mile. A major cremation site existed on the ridge, extending along the west bank of the river. At the town, an unusual mode of transportation was used to cross the river—a raft, made of bun-dles of tules tied together. This was propelled by Indian women who extended their legs through holes in the raft and with their feet maneuvered it from one shore to the other. It was on this type of craft that some of the early travelers and traders ferried their goods.

Eulalona was also a favored place for trading since it was located within traveling distance of many Indians on both sides of Upper Klamath Lake. It was only a short distance from the encampments on Lake Ewauna and the north shore of the Klam-ath River.

Mart Frain was an early trader in the region. He married a Shasta woman and lived in the Klamath Canyon near the Cali-fornia line. His son, Wren, told the writer that the signal sum-mons for a trading meeting was prepared by building three fires on the hill near the present site of Klamath Falls. These could be seen by the residents of Eulalona and all the way to the Lost River country to the southeast.

The house pits have now disappeared from the village site, but excavation for pipe lines or basements still occasionally brings remnants to the surface.

Winter Pit Houses

Pit houses were the winter homes of the Klamaths. They were quite different from the summer homes. In the standard winter house there were four posts supporting connecting beams in a square. From the beams, pole rafters were laid radially around the house with one end resting on the ground. To complete the structure, tule or cattail mats were placed over the rafters and covered with a layer of earth and rocks. The interior was dug out to a depth of from two to seven feet. Occupants entered from the roof and went down a ladder. This entrance also served as an escape for the smoke from the fire within.

Archeological research has produced proof of certain other features of these winter houses of the Klamaths: first, the pits usually had a saucer-shaped depression rather than a flat floor; second, the fire was located near the center of the house; third, the houses varied considerably in orientation and shape to suit the needs of the builder and to give easy access to the lake or stream; fourth, they varied considerably in size, as one was over fifty feet in diameter; fifth, broken bark and mats were placed upon the floors to help keep them dry. Excavations have revealed such variations as these: some houses lacked posts, and at least one had a side entrance. Instead of being round, some were oval shaped, and several of the pits had benches around the periphery.

To this day, there are still round and oval depressions where the winter houses of the Klamaths were built. In some places these are plainly visible, but in others close observation is required to find them. A few years ago, more than a hundred house pits could be counted at Little Wocas Bay at Klamath Marsh, and a few sites along Williamson River still show the pits. Some at Collier State Park on Highway 97 are scheduled for excavation so that visitors can view the ancient dwellings and their contents. The similarity of the Klamath houses to the pit houses of the early Southwest civilization offers an interesting study for archeologists.

Prehistoric Trade

U. S. Highway 97 crosses into Oregon from California near Klamath Falls, passes near Chiloquin, Bend, Redmond, and reaches the northern Oregon border near The Dalles. If a suitable name were given this interstate route, it could very well be "Redman's Route." It was along this same general course that the Indians carried on their commerce. Among the favored trade goods taken north by the Klamaths and Modocs were the slaves. At The Dalles, slaves were in good demand by the north coast and Lower Columbia River Indians—their commercial value being enhanced by the ease in transporting them.

The carved bone face shown in Fig. 98 is an example of another item of trade. About thumbnail size and fragmentary, it unquestionably had its origin in the mid-Columbia region. The crescents under the eyes, and the open mouth with teeth and extended tongue, mark it as typical of those found in the area of The Dalles. A research party from the University of California discovered a number of similar figurines there in 1930. They described the carvings as "very clean-cut and frequently so deep that the lines appear as bas-relief." They found the carvings only in association with cremations and concluded that they served a "primarily artistic or ceremonial purpose." A number of bone figurine fragments have been found by collectors in the same region since the original research.

The bone figurine pictured was found near the Williamson River at its confluence with Sprague River. It is totally unlike any carvings or pictures made in the Klamath country and is surely evidence of the traffic along "Redman's Route." The most interesting part of the story about this impudent-looking bone face must remain untold. What magic properties did its maker implant in it? What powers did it give its holder? Was it worn in the hair or carried away from the sight of the curious? What could the Klamath who possessed this talisman have traded for it? Was it worth a bride, a slave, or just a basket of wocas?

Fig. 98. Carved bone figurine—possibly Tsagaglalal from the Columbia.

Fig. 99. The stone and style suggest Mexico.

Other items which were traded to the Klamaths in prehistoric times were dentalia and olivella shells for use as beads. It is also likely that dried clams and salmon were carried along the Deschutes River for trade with the lake people. Salmon was the main product of the traders at The Dalles and would have been a logical part of any exchange.

Another prehistoric "trade" is believed to have taken place to bring the Klamaths the three-legged mortar shown in Fig. 99. This unusual pot was found by Paul Matthews near the Klamath Marsh when he was hunting deer. It had been thrown to the surface in the excavation for a gas line. The small pestle was inside the bowl, imbedded in a matrix of light, white soil common to that area. The writer was invited to examine the soil and the stone. Incredible as it may seem, the shape, type of stone, and type of pestle all point to Mexico as the probable source of this mortar. Perhaps the two-horned mano found in the Chama Valley was a part of the transaction for this three-legged mortar.

A few other mortars of this type have been taken from the Klamath Highland. Jim Kerns has a similar one of lava stone given to him by an Indian woman. Another was uncovered by the waters of Lost River. It is, of course, possible that these mortars were traded in historic times; but the conditions of their discovery and the related information leads to the belief that they were of prehistoric origin and were not made locally. Many centuries must have been required for the changes in ownership and travel necessary to move such an item of primitive commerce along its way.

Antiquity of the Klamaths

Lack of information about the three-legged mortar calls attention to other unanswered questions about the many campsites around Upper Klamath Lake and Klamath Marsh. Some of these sites are known to have been occupied in recent times, but others still hold the secret of the huge time span over which the marsh dwellers kept their kind alive.

Fig. 100. Different ages are indicated by the shapes of the arrowheads.

Fig. 101. This large pipe has been repaired by the early owner.

A site of great antiquity near Modoc Point was discovered by Leroy Gienger. In making a cut for an irrigation ditch, he unearthed a layer of occupation containing chipped pieces of fossilized bone implements, but he found no arrowheads. He kept careful records of the site and placed the artifacts in the Gienger Museum in Chiloquin for further study.

A land-leveling operation at Tulana Farms near Chiloquin unearthed another example of the antiquity of the Klamath people. Pieces from this early site can be seen in Fig. 100. The large, desert side-notches and leaf-type points in the bottom row are in marked contrast to the small Shoshonean-type pieces shown in the top row—locally called "Chiloquin Points." These latter are found on virtually every camping place of the Klamaths, but they were completely absent on the deeper site where the large ones were found. The brown-and-white point in the center is from the deep layer, as are the other leaf-shaped objects below the Chiloquin points. The two on the left appear to have been mounted upon a spear or dart; those at the right are more like knives. Such chipped objects give further credence to the theory that the ancestors of the Klamaths came from the desert region to the east.

Smoking Habits

The massive pipe in Fig. 101 also came from the same cut made at Tulana Farms. The break in the pipe was evidently made during manufacture. It was then repaired and still shows evidence of some adhesive, probably pitch. A crude ring has been incised upon the end as though to hold a string. It would require a strong man to get a smoke from this pipe, for it is 12½ inches long and weighs over 3 pounds. Fig. 102 shows another pipe from the same site; this pipe is also much larger than those typical of the Klamaths. The hole in the side seems to have been made purposely for an unknown reason.

Fig. 103 shows two tiny pipes made of black steatite. This stone, sometimes called soapstone, is a shiny, soft material, usu-

Fig. 102. The hole in this pipe appears to have been made purposely.

Fig. 103. Tiny steatite pipes.

Fig. 104. A variety of fish net weights.

ally black but sometimes in shades of pastel green. None of the soapstones are native to the Klamath country, but are believed brought in from Northern California. These small pipes must have been used with a bone or wooden stem since the size would make them uncomfortably hot to smoke.

Tobacco was the only type of plant that Indians of the Klamath Highland were said to propagate. It is easy to see why they were unwilling to put forth the effort to grow food crops when the streams and marshes were so productive of natural food. Like many other Indian tribes, they used several plants for smoking.

Margaret Knowles Small spent much of her lifetime collecting and classifying over five hundred plants native to the Klamath region. These pressed specimens make up the herbarium named for her in the Klamath County Museum. She reported that four of these plants were used by the Indians for smoking. One of these was called "coyote" tobacco, *nicotiana attenuata*. This genus, belonging to the nightshade family, was the one which was propagated; it was more widely used than any other native tobacco. A plant of the buckthorn family called "tobacco bush" (*ceanothus velutinus*) was used in the stone pipes. The other two plants were members of the heath family: pine manzanita, *arctoslaphylas nevadensis*; and green manzanita, *arctoslaphylas patula*. The latter two plants were called kinnikinnick by the natives and were smoked straight or mixed with other tobacco. The round leaf called kinnikinnick was said to have a marked effect upon the smoker. The writer, who has sampled wocas, ipos, tules, chokecherries, and mullet, has yet to muster sufficient courage to smoke kinnikinnick.

Ogden Describes the Klamaths

Although the inhabitants did not practice agriculture, most villages were quite permanent. Some which were located on streams seemed to be especially selected for fishing purposes. Two such villages were near the junction of the Sprague and Williamson rivers. Txa'lmakstant was on the latter stream, and the village on the Sprague was named Ktai'tupakski ("at the stand-ing rock"). This was a favored fishing place, especially in the spring. Here a rock dam was constructed on the bottom of the river. The barrier did not reach the surface; however, it caused the fish to come near the surface, where the Indians with their nettle-fiber nets could dip them out.

In historical times, the property belonged to an Indian who was called Tche'lo-ins by Gatschet. The difficulty in pronounc-ing the words of the Klamaths must have been considerable be-cause Samuel Clark called this same man, Chal-o-quin. Another version was used at the signing of the Treaty of 1864, when the name was written Chaloquenas. The town now located at the confluence of the streams has been named to honor this village chief, but it is spelled Chiloquin.

It was likely the site of Chiloquin where Peter Skene Ogden stopped to visit on December 5, 1826. Fortunately he made de-tailed observations because the adaptable and intelligent Klam-aths were soon influenced in their way of life by commerce with other Indians to the northwest (probably Molallas) as well as with white traders. Ogden mentioned that they already knew the value of beaver at the time of his arrival. His comments on the food, dress, and honesty of the wocas people are all worthy of quotation:

". . . the Indian village [was] a few huts but of a very large size, square made and flat at the top, composed of earth and roots, the door at the top, and the snake and the inmates go in and out at the same door at the top. They are well constructed for defense against arrows but are not proof against balls.

"In course of the day about 200 of them collected about our camp. They appear to live in dread of enemies, constantly wear-ing their arms. Their dress appears rather strange—their leggins being made of reeds, also their shoes of the same—well adapted for snow but would not answer in the summer season—there is scarcely a difference in the dress of the men and women—the latter are very ordinary while the former are generally fine stout looking men. We succeeded at trading at a cheap rate 40 dogs and some small fish, not more than two inches in length and far from being good.

"The two chiefs delivered in two traps that had been lost there last year by Mr. McDonald, with eight beavers. They informed us they had taken upwards of 30 but had traded them with the Willamette Indians. This is so much in favour of their honesty—and with this I shall also add an axe that was lost this day found by them and brought to me."

Dogs of the Klamaths

The good fortune of the Hudson's Bay men in procuring forty dogs saved their horses from being used as food and also enabled them to press farther south. Though roasted dog was a common item on the menu of most Indians, this was not generally true of either the Modocs or the Klamaths. The very abundance of dogs among them showed their aversion to eating canine flesh. Even starvation rarely forced them to consume such fare. It would be interesting to know if their attitude toward eating dog had any relationship to the coyote deity, Wa'shamtch.

The flesh of dogs was recognized as a necessity for sustenance by many of the early exploring and trapping parties. Though Lewis and Clark at first shunned the animals so eagerly consumed by their companions, the French-Canadians, their Journals indicate that by the time they neared the Pacific they had discovered that dog was a common and desirable food.

The number of dogs was so great around Klamath Lake that Ogden named it Dog Lake. One can imagine the delight of the Chiloquin village people on discovering that the useless animals, who consumed so much fish and barked so loudly at night, could be traded for such desirable items as blue-glass beads and thimbles. It is also easy to understand their reluctance at having the bearers of such heaven-sent goods leave before the primitive "Fidos" had all been traded.

The law of supply and demand became operative, however, and on January 13, 1827, when Ogden's party was in Modoc County, he made this entry in his Journal:

"We traded 10 dogs this day. The natives paid us a visit to the number of eighty; they are certainly a most numerous tribe and fortunately for us they are well inclined and have a good stock of dogs, but now they find we are dependent on them they have considerably increased their value, but still they are not dear. We procure at the following rate—4 rings for one, the same number of buttons or thimbles—and for a scalper, two. These are the only trading articles we have barter'd with them with the exception of few beads for their beaver—as for ammunition, being without fire arms they set no value."

Fishing Industry

Since Ogden's arrival at Chiloquin in December had not coincided with the fishing season there, the small, miserable fish traded were not typical of those in the regular diet of the Klamaths. When he arrived at the lake, he noted: "the small fish were taken with a basket or scoop net made of willows; both ends are parted and the middle open and wide."

The main fish, and the food that probably ranked with wocas for the subsistence of the tribe, was a type of sucker now called mullet. This fish is so unusual in species and habit that special laws have been enacted for its protection and utilization. The mature fish leave the lake in the month of the "ring finger"—late February or March. (The Indian months did not coincide with calendar months.) The spawning season lasts about a month; but unlike the salmon, mullet return to the lake following the deposit of their eggs.

Mullet, nearly as huge as silver salmon, were called carp by Ogden and said to be "as good as white fish." The species found in Klamath Lake differ from the Tule Lake mullet. Both species leave the lake only during the spawning season and they are bottom feeders. Charlie Ogle, who was born at Klamath Agency, said that Tule Lake mullet were far less bony than those taken from the Williamson River. They take neither bait nor troll and must be caught by net, spear, or other such devices. During the spawning runs they arrive in such quantities that a large supply could be accumulated and dried for later use.

Since the season for gathering wocas ended in September, and the main migratory flight of waterfowl passed on south in early December, it was a long wait for the season of the mullet. It is easy to imagine the joy which accompanied their appearance. The fish, which never surface in the lake, seem to jump jubilantly during their river excursion.

Fishing in the lake was a year-round activity, and while the catch did not compare in numbers with the mullet run, it was still a major industry. All lake village sites show evidence of it where the waves have chewed into the soft banks, exposing various types of net weights. Fig. 104 shows some of the great variety of shapes of net weights used by the lake fishermen. The one pictured second from the left, formed somewhat like a heart, is a distinct type and is thought to have been used as a drag weight on the nets pulled behind canoes. It seems strange that so few anchors of the Tule Lake type are found on Upper Klamath Lake.

The small weights shown in Fig. 105 average about three inches in length and one and a half inches in diameter. Most of this type are round and deeply grooved. Some collectors call these "dumbbell" sinkers. If one of these stones were found in the Southwest it would be considered a club head. Practically all are well finished but the indentation for the knot attachment, so common on the Columbia, is rarely found in this region.

Another method for taking the lake fish was by trolling a straight bone fishhook called a gorge (Fig. 106). The line was fastened in the middle of the bone and bait attached as shown in the center of the figure. After this entered the stomach of the quarry, the pull on the line would turn the hook out at the ends. A compound fishhook pictured by S. A. Barrett in the research

Fig. 105. Most common type of weight.

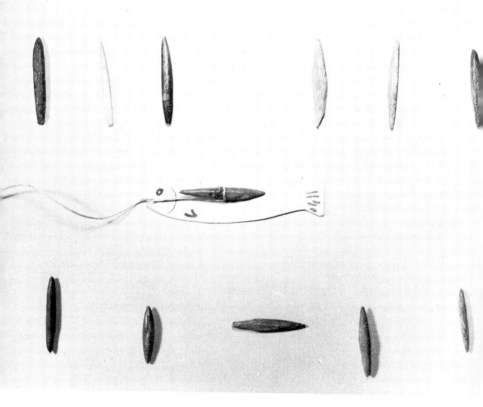

Fig. 106. Bone fish hooks.

report, *The Material Culture of the Klamath Lake and Modoc Indians*, has two straight bones attached to a shank. The bone in the middle of the lower row of Fig. 106 is probably a part of such a hook.

The bone harpoon is unknown on Upper Klamath Lake, but a distinctive type of arrowhead with long barbs is found at fishing sites (Fig. 107). Some collectors call these "Molly Points" in the belief that they were made by the Molalla Indians and traded into the Klamath region. There is no doubt that most of these long, barbed fishing points are made of imported material. Agate and jasper were generally used. Fragments of such stones are found scattered in abundance over the beaches near the fishing sites and seem to furnish adequate proof that, while the stones were imported, the manufacture took place at the site where the points were used. It could be that the gem-like material was easier to fashion into the long, delicate barbs favored for fishing. Another less likely explanation would be that the fish favored the more brightly colored points, and greater luck could be expected by using them. Members of the Siskiyou Archeological Society have made extensive collections of these gem points at the fishing sites in the Rogue River Valley.

Dr. Robert Heizer of the University of California has called these triangular long-eared arrowheads "Gunther points," after Gunther Island off the coast near Eureka, California. The shape is so distinctive that this type deserves a scientific name of its own. Gunther points have been found at fishing sites on the Trinity River as well as at the fishing villages throughout the Klamath and Rogue drainage system. It was the search for fish that led a modern fisherman to an interesting discovery on the Williamson River.

The Henwas

The Williamson and Sprague rivers both carry a considerable amount of dark humic material in the early spring. This is the result of the water passing through a marshy region before enter-

Fig. 107. Fishing points (Van Landrum photo)

Fig. 108. The Chiloquin henwas.

ing the canyons on the way to Klamath Lake. The Williamson heads in a clear spring but passes through the enormous Klamath Marsh. The Sprague has numerous other sources but is fed by the Sycan River, which also winds through the marsh by that name. Often in late June, the water level drops in both streams as the marshes empty and no longer feed in their brown waters. This is accompanied by a clearing and cooling in the stream below Chiloquin, where the rivers join. The large trout in Klamath Lake are drawn into these cooler waters as the lake warms.

Several years ago, Scott Warren, a Klamath County Commissioner, was likewise drawn to the confluence of the rivers; he hoped to take one of those big trout on a fly. Using a "flying caddis," tied especially for river fishing, Warren cast several times without success. Reeling in his line, he felt impelled to look down into the edge of the waters. There he noticed an algae-covered stone at a depth of about two feet. It was green like the other stones but had two sharp points on one end, divided by a notch.

Believing that the stone had been shaped by man rather than by nature, Warren decided that it was worth getting his shirt wet to have a closer look. After scraping the algae and encrustation of fresh-water mollusks off, he was puzzled by his find. During his occasional collecting and his service as a museum commissioner, no stone of this type had ever before come to his attention. He brought it to the Klamath County Museum for identification with the comment: "It looks like a stone idol." Warren did not realize how nearly right he was—he had found a henwas. He had also established positive proof that the henwas was not simply a family fetish handed down by a village group.

The museum curator, Roy Carlson, had had earlier experience with the henwas. He informed the writer in 1959 that there had been an opportunity to purchase all or part of the Lizzie Kirk collection of Indian stone objects, which included a number of unusual items shaped to resemble human beings. A money donation was solicited and a few of the stones were purchased. Carl-

Fig. 109. Family group of henwas.

Fig. 110. Male henwas. (Roy Carlson photo from Klamath County Museum)

son—who began an immediate search for information about the sculptured stones—determined from both Indian informants and linguistic studies that they were called by the name "henwas." A rough interpretation of the word is "rock standing upright." His report was presented at the Spokane meeting of the Professional Anthropologists and was published in the *American Anthropologist* for June 1959.

The stones were supposedly used by the Indian doctors in their various rites and possessed mysterious qualities. They were shaped according to sex. Males and females were sometimes found together.

Lizzie Kirk told Curator Carlson that her husband found a pair on the bank of Williamson River. Being afraid, he tossed them into the river. When he returned later, they were again on the shore. She said that the shaman doctors used them in curing disease.

Despite the evidence presented by Carlson and my respect for his sincerity, I still questioned the general use of the henwas by the Indian people. Thirty years in the Klamath region have brought me into association with so many unusual artifacts and interesting stories about them that all are regarded with skepticism. Why was the henwas not more widespread in distribution? Why had only Indians found them? Why only at the mouth of the Williamson River?

The discovery by Scott Warren (Fig. 108) provided an answer to all of these questions. Since Carlson's paper was presented, three additional finds of the henwas have been reported. Fig. 109, from the Kirk collection, shows the Warren henwas between two female relatives. They now calmly stare back at the visitors in the Klamath County Museum. Those shown in Fig. 110 can be distinguished as males by the notch at the top, the lack of breasts, and by the stubby arms.

The notched top on the mauls in Fig. 111 gives them a henwas-like character. They lack any other feature of the stone

Fig. 111. Mauls notched in the manner of a henwas.

Fig. 112. Deep-water canoe near Harriman Lodge. (From Maude Baldwin Collection in Klamath County Museum)

idols, however, and are more likely to have been used in the wocas or canoe industry.

The Canoe Industry

The Canadian goose and a few species of ducks spend the entire year in the Klamath region. Most varieties are migratory and start the fall migration into the basin in August. The most welcome arrivals for the Indians were the spring migrants who came to lay their eggs. An egg is much easier to obtain than a duck; besides, it has no feathers, so is much easier to prepare. A canoe, however, is necessary, for in the spring the waters are high in both the lake and marshes. A canoe industry, second to none, permitted the Lake People to gather this bountiful harvest, the use of which was ultimately woven into the fabric of their daily life. A typical deep-water canoe, much longer than the marsh boat, is shown in Fig. 112.

Mauls and wedges were a part of the canoe industry, and while many of the bone wedges have decayed, the maul remains a common artifact left by the lake people. Fig. 113 shows two types of mauls tilted at an angle to make the bottoms visible. The one on the right has a slight knob at the top; the bottom is cupped from use. The maul at the left is more typical of the Klamath bell-bottom type.

Fig. 114 illustrates several types of tools made of antler. Those at the top (No. 1) are typical wedges which have been used with a maul. The other horn specimens are so shaped that they were used for other purposes, possibly for removing either the fat or the hair from animal skins. No. 3 (in the center of the picture), although badly disintegrated, shows the remains of decorative designs and has a hole bored through it, possibly for attaching a thong for carrying the implement. Certainly neither the decoration nor the hole would have been put on an elk horn if its use had been for a wedge.

In Fig. 115, the wedges numbered 2 and 4 are typical elk-horn wedges from Lower Klamath Lake. The bone specimens in

Fig. 113. Bell-bottom and concave-bottom maul. The maul on the right was dug out by pet springer spaniel.

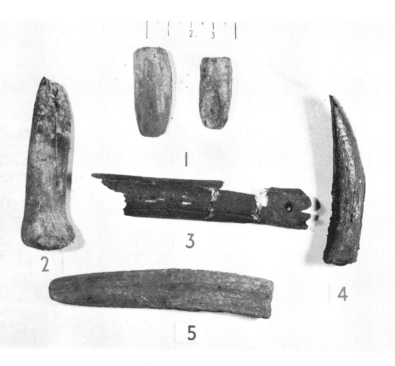

Fig. 114. Deer and elk-horn tools.

Fig. 115. Gouges of bone with antler wedges.

Fig. 116. An alkali crust has formed on some of these "potato-masher" type mauls.

Fig. 117. The use made of these tiny mauls is puzzling.

the upper part (No. 1) are gouges. They have a rather sharp cutting edge and could well have been used for gouging the charcoal from the burned interior of a log in the process of constructing a canoe. The sharp, pointed bones (No. 3) have a V-shaped end. Their use is unknown.

Neither the long salmon-packer mauls nor the mauls with the animal-shaped tops, such as were found on the Columbia River, are found in the Klamath Highland. Many mauls resemble pestles with one blunt end. Another type, with a potato-masher shape like those in Fig. 116, is found in both the desert area and the Klamath lakes country. The author once found three of these buried beneath a metate near Silver Lake.

It is difficult to understand the purpose of the small mauls in Fig. 117. The smallest is only three inches high. Possibly the tops of the mauls were used like a pestle as grinders in a mortar, and the wide end served only such purposes as were incidental to the use of the pestle. The bell-bottom mauls, while fairly common in the Klamath area, are virtually unknown in the Paiute country.

The canoe helped make it possible for the Klamath people to establish permanent villages, since they were able to secure enough food by traveling their water courses. The establishment of the permanent village in turn enabled them to develop a much more sophisticated religious life and more unwritten legends than their nomadic Paiute neighbors to the east.

Religion and Superstition

The religious life and the everyday life of the Klamath were so interwoven that it would be impossible to separate the two. The appearance of a bird or the disappearance of a deer would likely be attributed to the work of the mighty deity K'mukamtch, or to his trickster son called Ai'shish. Likewise, if the geese unexpectedly took flight during a stalking expedition, the act might be attributed to Wa'shamtch of the Many Voices (coyote). The winds, which came from nowhere and were made of nothing, evoked the feeling of superstitious wonderment. Certain mountains were credited with power over winds. The tapping on certain rocks by the shaman was also supposed to create weather conditions. Powers were attributed to certain stones and great value was placed upon them. The power stones in Fig. 118 are all imported from outside the area; some are crystals, others are coastal agates. Many show wear from being carried by their owners for years. Such power stones or good luck stones have also been found by the writer in the Hohokam sites of Arizona and in Mexico.

In several places there were natural rock formations which were believed to possess supernatural powers. The story of one of these, Tgawalsh (pronounced Tuckwalla), was told to Alfred Collier, long-time lumberman and collector of Indian stories, who related it to the author. Tuckwalla, shown in Fig. 119, was located on the Sprague River near Beatty, Oregon. This rock seems to have served as a stone psychiatrist. In order to receive the maximum benefits, the Indian who had a problem first had to achieve a good and happy frame of mind—which may not have been easy with an empty stomach. He could then visit Tuckwalla and tap him on the shoulder three times to get his attention. The problem could then be related to Tuckwalla. If everything was done properly, and a small reward such as a few ipos was left, the answer to the problem would come to the patient at a later time. Such stone psychiatric services, without benefit of couch, doubtless helped many unfortunates arrive at a happy frame of mind.

Another geological feature with certain religious importance is a large rock in Sprague River about four miles from Chiloquin, called Medicine Rock. Klamath Indians believed it had special supernatural power to cure illness.

Many of the legends and myths of the Indians had some religious meaning, but the line between the entertainment value and the religious significance is difficult to draw. For the modern man to understand the importance that story telling had for the In-

Fig. 118. Crystals and agates, traded in from outside areas, were valued for their power as well as beauty.

Fig. 119. Tgawalsh (pronounced Tuckwalla), the stone psychiatrist. (Alfred Collier photo)

dian, it is necessary to imagine a society in which there is no written word, no radio communication, no professional entertainment, and no schools to pass along the knowledge and heritage of the race. As means of expression and entertainment, this left only the story, the dance, the healing arts, and gambling.

The healing practices by the shaman were often audience-participation events and had a definite religious or magic effect, with some entertainment thrown in. Luck, as we call it, entered not only into gambling, but into many ordinary events. In the case of the Indian, a better word than luck would have been power, because most thought that some type of positive or negative power was part of each circumstance, whether it was gambling, warfare, or hunting. Add to this belief the continuing state of anxiety in which the Klamaths lived because of the normal hazards of their lives, and it is possible to see why they sought all means of gaining supernatural power for protection and help.

The principal deity of the Klamath Indians was K'mukamtch, who had all the virtues and vices of his human admirers, plus unlimited powers. In his love affairs and battles he usually took the form of an animal or bird, and he always recovered from his many deaths. His problems were a magnification of the problems of men. Each time a new story was told around the fire of a winter lodge, a new twist or angle could be added by the teller in order to heighten the entertainment value. As a result, the legends of K'mukamtch and his son, Ai'shish, who was also his principal competitor, would be limited only by the number of tellers.

Gatschet, who collected the stories for the Smithsonian Institution, reported hundreds of legends in the unwritten Lutuami language. Whether or not these stories had a religious significance, or merely entertainment value, would depend upon the attitude of both narrator and listener. By the time of Gatschet's arrival, the biblical influence had entered the legends in the story of a man and woman living together in harmony until the woman ate the forbidden berries as a result of the influence of the power of evil.

Animal guardians were often regarded as a source of individual help, protection, or power, in meeting the normal problems of life. Sometimes inanimate objects or growing things would be recognized as a source of luck or assistance; this was especially true in the work of the conjurer or shaman. The way to become a shaman was to have the right dream of the power source, compose the proper songs, then properly convince others that performances would bring results. In this way new context could be added to the religious or medical lore with each generation. Results were the measure of success in the practice of the conjurer; and if failure to bring a cure should result in death of the patient, the relatives of the deceased might feel entitled to assess heavy indemnities against the practitioner, or even kill him.

The Power Quest

Power was sought not only by the shaman but by each individual. At about the time of puberty, boys and sometimes girls would go to an isolated place, a high cliff, a cave, or mountain on a power quest. By doing without food, by piling rocks in piles, by bathing and staying under water for a long period, they sought to have a dream or vision. The results of the dream would determine which animal or object was to be the source of their luck or power thereafter. Piles of rocks are still on a cliff overlooking the Williamson River near Kirk as a result of such quests. A small, deep cave near Bonanza, marked by two pictographs, was believed by Joe Meeker to be the site of a power quest. This cave could more accurately be described as a hole—it is almost perfectly round and only large enough to accommodate a human body. Lack of water, food, or any other attraction in the vicinity would almost certainly indicate that its only use was as one of the sacred places.

An instance where the just and powerful deities of the Indian were called upon was told to the writer by Alfred Collier. In this case, a labor dispute at Fort Klamath was settled by the gods, but not in a manner entirely satisfactory to management.

According to "Cap" Collier's account, an early-day rancher named Melhase had hired, among others, an Indian doctor or conjurer named Lee Snipe. The native crew was employed to harvest the grassy meadow hay and then pile it into stacks for the feeding of the cattle during the winter season. Snipe, who lived on Link River, derived his particular power from ducking under water and holding his breath for long periods of time.

It is impossible to imagine the type of visions which came to him during the breathless periods under water. We know, however, that he had a method of impressing prospective clients with his power that was as unique as it was effective.

The warm stone walls of the Link River Canyon, together with the abundant supply of frogs and minnows, made the shores an attractive place for water snakes. These black-and-yellow reptiles, also called garter snakes, would group together and "ball up" in bunches in the spring season. Snipe would emerge from his under-water seance with the spirits, then—filled with power— he would dive stark naked on his stomach into a pile of the writhing snakes. Doubtless this display of disdain for the unpleasant had the effect of convincing even the more skeptical doubters of his courage and capability.

In some manner, at the Melhase ranch, Snipe had incurred the displeasure of his employer and was discharged from his job. He promptly threatened that if he were not rehired that he would make them sorry. When his threat was laughed off, the conjurer found a mud spring at the foot of the Cascade Range. Sitting upon the ground before the spring, he broke small sticks into pieces, meanwhile invoking the wrath of the gods upon Melhase. His prayers and incantations were uttered as he cast the broken sticks into the waters of the spring.

Shortly after Snipe's lonely ceremony, dark clouds started to form around the sides of Mt. McLoughlin, while violent drafts of wind sent them billowing and surging into great white domes in the sky. Winds funneling between peaks of the Cascades pushed the storm out past Seven Mile Creek and over the green meadows of the Fort Klamath country. The vengeance of the Indian doctor was then expressed in terms of thunder, lightning, and torrents of rain.

The freshly raked and shocked hay was completely wet and likely to spoil unless something was done. Snipe returned to reason with Melhase, certain in his belief that if the rancher was not convinced of the justice of his cause, he would be aware of his power.

It seems that Melhase was not only unwilling to return the Indian to the haying job, but was unimpressed by the storm. He stubbornly attributed it entirely to natural causes rather than to the supernatural. Further, he was downright discourteous to Snipe. Melhase used the plain language that was often employed by angry frontiersmen when giving vent to angry thoughts. Ignoring Snipe's plea, he simply ordered his crew to turn the dampened piles of hay over with pitchforks to allow them to dry in the wind and sun.

It was with a heavy heart that Snipe returned to the mud spring. Seldom had he failed to convince others of his special relationship with those who directed the elements. Again he sat by the spring to break the sticks. Again he cast them into the spring and invoked the help of the Indian spirits. Again the clouds formed over the Cascades and violent winds roared through the pines. Again lightning split the skies and the thunder reverberated over the entire Wood River Valley.

When the rain came this time, it fell on hay that had already received a soaking from the previous storm. The new growth of meadow hay was starting to send shoots into the recently turned mounds of hay.

No one knows the conversation that took place when Snipe returned a second time to his former employer. It must have been hard for Melhase to put the Indian doctor back on the payroll, for the rancher was a proud man. Perhaps it was because of sympathy for the wintering cattle. More likely, Melhase simply became convinced of the power of the medicine man. In any case, the first job security was thus established in the Klamath country, and the Melhase family prospered and became one of the prominent pioneer families.

One of the most widely circulated stories regarding the taboos of the Klamath Indians is the one about Crater Lake. It has been told and retold that the Klamaths had a great fear of Crater Lake and could not be induced to go near it. The origin of the story is not known and may have been due only to the fact that this high lake was entirely out of the habitat of these Indians. Selden Kirk, long the distinguished head of the Klamath Tribal Council, informed the writer that the story was groundless. He said that when he was a boy, he and a friend had descended into the 2,000-foot crater and had taken a swim in the lake.

The Indians' lack of interest in this beautiful body of water probably lies in the fact that it contained neither fish nor game and required such a long, steep descent in soft pumice to reach the water. Add to this the possibility of an arrow from the bow of an unfriendly Umpqua Indian — then the taboo takes on a meaning not based on religion but on common sense.

Unlike the religion of some tribes, the religion of the Klamaths did not forbid the adoption of new ideas, nor intermarriage with the white people. As a result, the transition to modern living has been comparatively rapid and has enabled the tribal people to accept Christian concepts while still remaining unconquered. They have also been quick to accept the dress, houses, and educational methods of the newcomers. Though their adaptation to modern society has not been without problems, it has certainly been much smoother than that of the Navajo and Hopi Indians, with their more conservative and fixed religious beliefs.

As Clear Lake lowered, the churning waves carried the soil away, leaving the exposed rocks where the Indians had camped. Carr Butte in the distance was named for the family that purchased the Clear Lake ranch from the Applegates.

5. THE LOST RIVER CIRCLE

The River That Disappeared

The name of Lost River fits the stream perfectly, and it seems fortunate that the name McCrady River, bestowed upon the stream by Colonel Fremont in 1846, did not last. Some say that Lost River was given its name because it flows in a circuitous route for ninety miles and ends near its source. Others have said that it was called "lost" because the identity of the river disappeared as it entered the marsh in Langell Valley, then took shape again when the water left the valley. In any case, the banks and islands of the stream, along its entire course, have been a camping place for Indians over a period of many centuries.

The favored places for villages seemed to be where there were riffles in the river or where a spring fed into a stream. Such conditions existed at the Hot Springs in Langell Valley, Big Springs at Bonanza, the Horton Ranch at Dairy, Harpole Dam, Olene, Stukel Point, and Merrill. There was, of course, the large village above the outlet of the river at Tule Lake, where the first shots of the Modoc War were fired in later years. Many smaller springs and islands made the banks an almost continuous area of occupation all along the meandering course. Each year, as the farmers till the soil of the valley, stone utensils and chipped objects continue to be brought to the surface.

One of the sites still occupied into historic times was the village just below Lost River Gap, near the present town of Olene. This site had a number of features which made it most desirable as a living place. The rapids in the river made it ideal for taking fish by spear or net; a number of hot springs occurred where the channel of the river cut through the hills at Olene; and finally, a warm creek flowing from Crystal Springs into the river provided an ice-free location for waterfowl to alight during the cold winter season when lakes and streams elsewhere were frozen.

Lost River Mullet Run

By treaty with the United States Government, Modoc Indians were required to remain within the bounds of the Klamath Indian Reservation unless issued a travel permit—but the treaty did not remove from the Modocs the firmly ingrained habits of many centuries.

In the spring of the year they were permitted to return to their favorite fishing spot on Lost River. A picture taken in 1898 shows a group encampment at the Lost River Gap (Fig. 120). The well-dressed ladies beside the harnessed carriage-horse undoubtedly accompanied the photographer, Maude Baldwin. The steep Olene Ridge in the background is marked on the top by rock cairns and circles made by the adolescent braves on their "power quest" journeys. The ridge also was a favored crossing place for mule deer during the annual fall migration to the Lava Beds. It is understandable that old yearnings as well as wildlife would incite the people to migrate.

Strangely enough, the Lost River mullet they sought was a different species from that in Klamath Lake, and both were different from the mullet in Winnemucca Lake in Nevada. The fish would leave Tule Lake at the time of the snow runoff in late February or March. The spawning run of the Lost River mullet must have been a sight to behold. Ada Grigsby Brown, who lived at Olene when she was a little girl, said that the surging fish so filled the river that farmers could back their wagons into the

Fig. 120. Indians return to Lost River near Olene for their mullet camp.

Fig. 121. These drying racks of willows are loaded.

stream and fill them in a short time by using a pitchfork to scoop the fish out of the water.

Attracted by the economic potential of the fish, a Mr. Whitman from Medford established a cannery on the island below Olene in 1892. He packed the fish in tin cans for the market and also prepared them by drying.

In historic times, Indians have taken the fish with a steel hook on the end of a willow pole, according to Charles Drew, who owned the ranch where the Modocs fished. He also mentioned the use of a triple-tined spear on a willow pole. The fish were cleaned by Indian women and dried on racks as shown in Fig. 121. The dress of the Indian and his mode of travel had changed in 1898, when these pictures at Lost River Gap were taken, but the excitement which accompanied the gathering was the same as in centuries past. The happiness and social significance of the occasion could be rivaled perhaps by the Mardi Gras.

To the early Modocs, the coming of mullet in the spring meant many things. First in importance was the sharp call of hunger. After a season when nothing grows except children and appetites, the rich, oily fish could mean comfort and even survival. The social importance was also great; an abundant food supply could make possible a gathering together of people, which was a luxury seldom afforded those who lived off the land. In their stern competition over the land's offerings, they were forced to remain apart much of the year; but at the great seasonal gatherings, old friendships were renewed and new tales were related around the sagebrush fires. Of prime importance also was the gambling. Nights would then ring with the rhythmic tap-tap-tap-tap of the stick-game players as they sought to get their adversaries to betray the whereabouts of the polished bone.

The mullet was not the only fish to be taken in Lost River. Trout, chub, and minnow were also available. The numbers of net weights found along the shores attest to the importance of these lesser species of fish. Fresh-water mussels were undoubtedly a source of food along the muddy bottom of the river and in the headwaters of Clear Lake.

Clear Lake in Modoc County

If the name Lost River fits the stream, the name Clear Lake must have been applied with tongue in cheek, for it is anything but clear. In its original state, prior to artificial controls, it could hardly have been clear, as the bottom in many places consisted of the same black humus characteristic of the marshes in the Klamath country. The lake lies entirely in Modoc County, California, and is fed by Willow Creek, plus many springs, some submerged and some around the shores. It must have been an attractive place for the cattle industry because a number of the earliest pioneer families settled along its shores.

It is difficult to determine where the original shore of Clear Lake was located because the construction of the dam at the outlet has caused the water depth to fluctuate over fifteen feet, depending upon wet and dry years. The rainfall in the Clear Lake-Lost River watershed is smaller in amount and less to be depended on than the waters which flow from the Cascades into Upper and Lower Klamath Lake. As a result of this uncertainty in the amount of rainfall, plus the holding power of the dam, a barren, almost biological desert has been created around the shores. It was a naturally shallow lake, much of it marsh in its original state. The water fluctuation has made it devoid of plant life and caused severe erosion.

The barren scene stretching for miles in all directions imparts an eerie feeling to those who visit Clear Lake. One lady said that she felt as though the Indians were about to come back to get revenge upon her because she was visiting their old sanctuary.

Water is the active force on Klamath Lake and wind is the active force in the Fort Rock area. The wind also blows hard at Clear Lake but ice, too, has been a powerful force. Prior to the construction of an artificial dam at the Lost River outlet, the same natural level of Clear Lake was maintained each season. The winter's ice would form to a considerable thickness, then when the spring breakup occurred, the strong prevailing winds forced the ice into the gently sloping shores. As it pushed into the sandy soil, the action was similar to a great, long bulldozer pushing the soil ahead of it.

Centuries of this action created long ridges called ice dikes paralleling those lake shores away from prevailing winds. Since these long, narrow islands were higher than the surrounding marsh, they were highly desirable sites for the camps of the native inhabitants. The full extent of occupation might never be known were it not that the control dam had been built for irrigation. This structure has caused great changes in the water level. Sometimes the dikes, which once protruded, are under twelve feet of water; during arid cycles they may be extremely dry and joined to the shore by land. Under certain rainfall conditions, the water and ice level is the right depth to cause the ice to shear away the soil of the islands that it once built. This exposes the old camping places of the Indians.

It is not possible to tell the exact depth that the erosion has cut, but the implements, weapons, and burials of the former inhabitants were uncovered, moved, and covered again as the natural elements carried out their work (Fig. 122). In some places rocks and boulders weighing fifty to seventy pounds have been moved into neat lines in a row along the shore. The movement of the soil has been so great that it is now impossible to estimate the original depth of burials or artifacts. As they become unearthed in one place, they become buried more deeply in another. My observation of this erosive force over a period of thirty years has revealed many interesting characteristics of the people who built their lives, generation upon generation, out of the resources and climate of the Lost River Circle.

Stone Work of the Lost River Circle

It is called the Lost River Circle because of the route taken by Lost River from Clear Lake to the north, the west, and then

Fig. 122. Ice and waves have un-earthed this early resident.

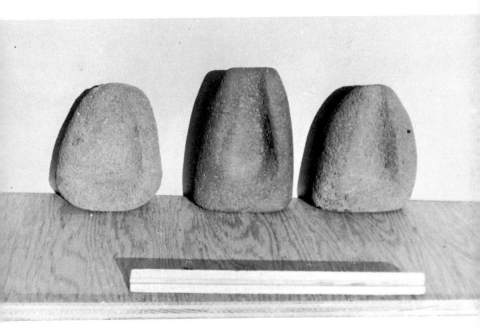

Fig. 123. These strangely shaped stones resemble huge kernels of corn.

back to the south, ending in Tule Lake. The stones and material culture found along this Circle have a certain relationship or "alikeness" that archeologists might call a Lost River complex. Many of those who have collected and studied the artifacts of the region agree that these also show differences from those of the Tule Lake and Lower Klamath Modocs.

The stone objects in Fig. 123 are found in the Lost River Circle but are exceedingly rare in other areas. A number of uses has been suggested for these interesting pieces, but none has been proved. The name "medicine stone" was applied by the late Ken McLeod, who thought that the side of the object was used to grind the medicinal materials such as bark, berries, or roots. Others have suggested that they were used as a type of maul, but they do not show the wear normally expected from such a use. The indentations are on both sides of the stones.

Fig. 124 shows a series of stones illustrating a possible developmental sequence in the invention of the "medicine stone." At the far left is an ordinary anvil used as a base for pounding or chipping. The series pictured here shows progressively more refinement; note the nice pouring spout on the stone at the far right.

Another type of object found in the Lost River Circle, but rarely in other places, is the stone shaped like a fan or paddle (Fig. 125). A site in Langell Valley has produced many of these fan-shaped rocks. A few from Clear Lake and from Sycan Marsh have also been reported. The restricted use suggests that a specialized food process may have accounted for them.

The roller-shaped stones in Fig. 126, called mauls by some, are frequently discovered in the Lost River Circle, but are rare elsewhere. Several have been found in the Kawumkan Springs excavation. The largest of these are too heavy and improperly shaped to make good mauls. The late Joe Meeker, who studied the camps and stones of Clear Lake for many years, thought they could have been foot pestles for crushing ipo roots or other fresh, succulent-type foods, possibly in one of the unshaped mortars.

Fig. 124. The stone anvil on the left may have been the predecessor of the medicine stone.

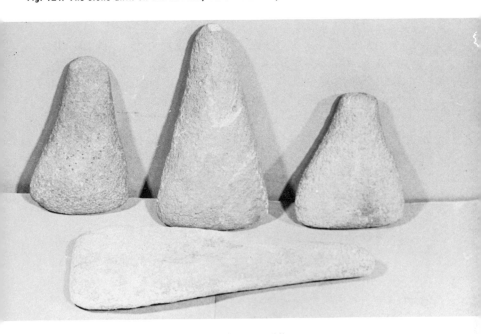

Fig. 125. Stone fans or paddles.

Fig. 126. Large-diameter grinders or foot pestles.

Another curious type of artifact reported in the Lost River Circle, but not in other places, is the star-shaped rock in Fig. 127. These are called mace heads and are a part of the Meeker family collection. The wooden handle would have been fitted into the hole, making it an effective club. The shiny, drilled stone on the left in Fig. 128 is from Warner Valley. It shows wear on the ends indicating use as a club. The club in the center of the picture and the chipped axe head are both from Christmas Valley and were found by Elvine and Roy Gienger. The hammer-shaped stone at the far right could be either a club head or a net weight. The ends are much flatter than those normally found on weights.

Stone Frying Pans?

Among the most unusual and interesting utensils from the Lost River Circle are the "frying pans" shown in Figs. 129, 130, and 131. There has been considerable conjecture regarding the purpose of these handled objects because they seem to be found in no other Indian cultures in Oregon or the Southwest. However, they have certain common characteristics which suggest their use as lamps. First, they are always made of a type of stone which could stand heat, usually some porous material. Nearly all show signs of fire around the bowl portion.

The Indians of Alaska used lamps in which they burned fish oil. Their lamps were commonly made of soapstone and were frequently oval in shape like the stones pictured. However, the northern lamps were thinner, and a notch was usually present to hold the moss wick. They had no handles but occasionally a long end.

If the stone "frying pans" are lamps, it will mark them as a significant discovery because they have not been reported from other areas in the continental United States. William H. Holmes, of the Bureau of American Ethnology, wrote: "It is a remarkable fact that the lamp is unknown in any other part of America (except Alaska), while several forms are found in arctic Asia."

Fig. 127. Stone mace heads.

Fig. 128. Clubs, mace, and axe heads.

Fig. 129. Porous material was usually selected for frying pans.

Fig. 130. Stones from Clear Lake found by the Meeker family.

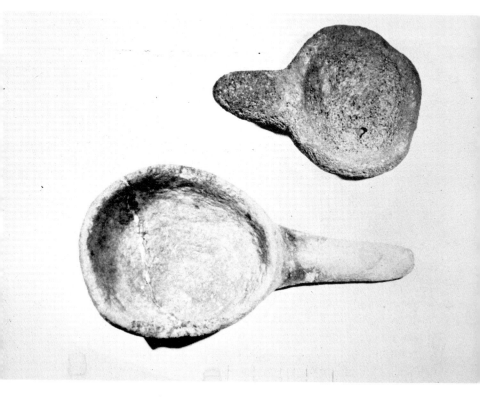

Fig. 131. Frying-pan-shaped stones thought to be lamps.

One professional archeologist, who was shown the stones and consulted on the problem, agreed that they were lamps but did not want to state so positively without more substantial proof. While these items are rare, there have been enough of them found to prevent their being classified as freaks or eccentrics. In addition to those found at Clear Lake, a few other localities have yielded evidence of their use. Gene Favell found one on Lower Klamath Lake, and the author found one in the bank of the Klamath River near Klamath Falls. It seems entirely possible that the native inhabitants of the Klamath Highland learned to use the oils of the mullet or salmon in a way similar to their Alaskan cousins.

It is difficult to account for the variety and difference of the objects left by the Lost River Circle people in contrast with objects found at other Modoc sites such as Tule Lake or Lower Klamath. One possible explanation is that the Lost River artifacts represent a different age and thus a different stage of development in the Modoc culture. Joe Meeker reported that the best materials came to the surface at Clear Lake only following some years of erosion, after the wind and ice had had a chance to cut deeply into the soils of the old villages. He theorized that the same archeological materials would be found at Tule Lake and other Modoc sites if the forces of erosion were to cut to the depth occupied by the more ancient people.

In addition to the possibility of a greater age, another reason for the variation in the cultural remains of the Lost River Circle could be its location in relation to other Indian tribes. In historic times, the Clear Lake Modocs had common frontiers with the Snakes of Goose Lake Valley, the Klamaths, and the Pit Rivers or Achomawi. They also may have ranged into the hunting territory of the Shastas in pursuit of deer or elk. In ancient times an even greater variety of neighbors could have influenced them. With more common borders, a greater exchange of ideas would normally take place. This, in turn, could stimulate the copying or production of a wider variety of arts and products—a sort of melting pot of people.

Chipped Objects

The two small arrowpoints at the top of Fig. 132 serve to illustrate the borrowing of material culture items from a neighboring tribe, or of trading with them. The notches on the backs resemble those found in Nevada, though this style is seldom found on Modoc sites. The prevailing type of projectile point seems to confirm the greater age of the Lost River Circle culture. The desert side-notch points are much more abundant, although often more crudely made, than the later triangular Gunther type. The pieces in the row above the smaller knife resemble Warner Valley points more than those of the nearby Tule Lake Basin.

The knife shown at the bottom of Fig. 132 is the Jim DeVore knife, the longest found in this area—thirteen and a half inches long. It was discovered where ice and wave action had exposed a burial. Its presence at Clear Lake suggests the borrowing of yet another practice from a neighboring tribe, the Shastas. Both the Indians on the Rogue River and those in Siskiyou County carried on the ceremonial dance of the white deerskin and displayed their treasured, giant obsidian blades. The DeVore blade could qualify for such a ceremony, although there is no proof that it was so used.

It is extremely difficult to take a broken fragment from a large knife and estimate the original length. So many blades are almost oval in shape that width is no positive indication. Enough broken fragments of large knives have been found on the shores of Clear Lake to provide strong evidence of the ceremonial use of these objects.

Great Variety of Pipes

The modified two-horned mano was borrowed from the Klamaths. Another item which must have been borrowed—and from many sources—was the pipe. The Lost River Circle seems un-

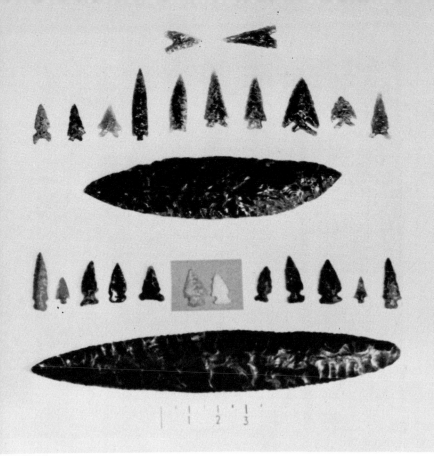

Fig. 132. Chipped objects from the Lost River Circle, showing the longest knife found in the area.

Fig. 133. Red-stone angle pipe.

rivaled in the great size, shape, and variety of pipes that have been found there. They have not, however, been numerous— the writer hunted for eleven years before finding one. But in terms of variety, the inventiveness of the makers was great. This again seems to indicate a long period of occupation and considerable antiquity. Fig. 133 shows an angle pipe, one of three found in a cache on Lost River by Albert Wilkinson. One of the set was only partially drilled, indicating that the stone was probably imported before it was manufactured. The material is red sandstone. The holder of the pipe is now a dentist, Dr. Lyle Haley of Grants Pass.

Fig. 134 shows three pipes on loan to the Klamath County Museum. These are made of a fine white sandstone, and the one on the left has been burned. The center pipe was found on the Percy Dixon ranch near Lost River. A hole had been drilled in it as though for carrying it on a cord.

The term "cloud blower," which originated in the southwestern United States, designates a short, thick pipe reportedly used for ceremonial purposes, during which the bowl was held to the lips and smoke was blown throughout the room much like incense. The one pictured in Fig. 135 completely disputes this theory. The small end of the pipe contains the remains of a bird-bone stem. The stem would reduce the difficulty of smoking to the point of making it suitable for one who had the habit. Smoking by the Indians was undoubtedly of both social and ceremonial significance, but the writer is of the opinion that the smokers generally had the habit. Further evidence to support this view is presented in another chapter.

The two angle pipes shown in Fig. 136 are the longest and among the most highly decorated of any found in this region. The bottom pipe is twenty-one inches in length (outer measurement), and is made of pale green steatite or soapstone. The carving extends around the pipe and the lines intersect, resulting in a series of squares on the surface. The bore comes to the surface

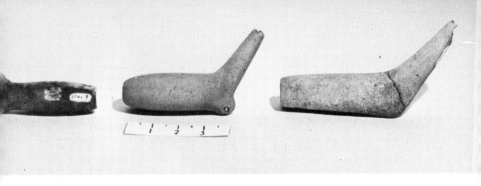

Fig. 134. The middle pipe has a hole for string.

Fig. 135. A piece of bird-bone stem was found in this cloud blower.

Fig. 136. Two large angle pipes.

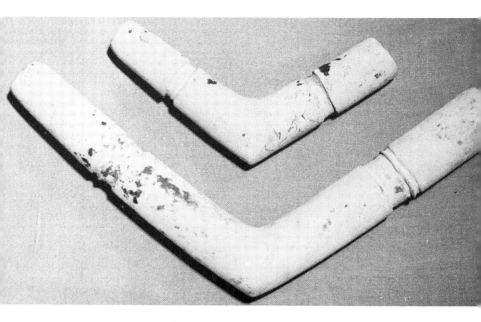

Fig. 137. White-stone angle pipes found together.

at the elbow. The smoother appearance of the stone at this point makes it look as though it had been wrapped with some substance such as buckskin to make it draw properly. Both pipes were found in a washed-out burial site by Jim Thomas of Klamath Falls. The upper pipe is of smooth, brown stone with a slight ridge along the top. The ridge has been notched at one-fourth-inch intervals to give an added aesthetic effect. This pair of fine pipes is remarkable not only for size but for symmetry, and the stone is of such quality that they qualify as art objects as well as archeological specimens. The other pieces in the frame include a bone spoon (at the top), deerhorn wedges (lower left), and a number of bone and chipped objects.

The angle pipe seemed to reach its zenith in Lost River Circle. Fig. 137 from the Meeker Collection shows a pair found close together. A fine white sandstone seems to be the material used. In Fig. 138, the girl makes the pipe look better and illustrates the size.

The bone and wooden stems used on pipes were fitted to the stone portion in two different ways. Fig. 139 illustrates a type of fitting in which the bone is attached to the interior of the stem. The pipe at the left, from Clear Lake, has three sets of carved marks upon the bowl similar to the set showing in the picture. The bone tube inserted in the pipe was not found in place but on the surface nearby.

The source of stone for the pipes would make a fine study for the expert in geology because there is such a great variety of material. Some, of course, are made of the local volcanic material but most are from substances found outside the region. It is entirely possible that the large-angle pipes were developed locally rather than being traded from neighboring tribes, because the shape and size seem unmatched elsewhere. One large pipe found along Lost River in Poe Valley was made of imported stone, but the boring of the center was incomplete—a sure indication that manufacture was local.

Fig. 138. Should a lady smoke an angle pipe?

Fig. 139. (below) These bowls were probably used with bone or wood tubes.

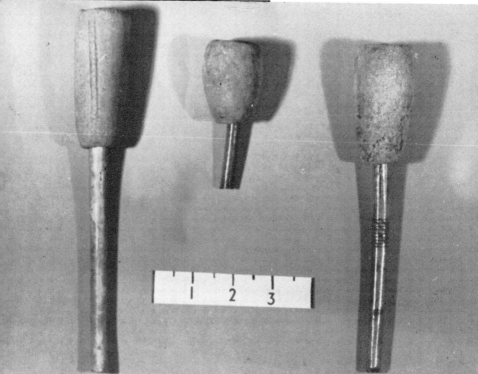

Objects of Clay

With trade being carried on between Indian tribes as extensively as it was, it would normally be expected that all Indians would practice the art of pottery-making. For two reasons this was not the case in the Modoc country of Northern California and Oregon. First, pottery is fragile and not easily moved about. These semi-nomadic people found hide and basketry containers more practical for their way of life. However, in the areas where primitive people developed agriculture, and were thus enabled to establish permanent homes, pottery development was natural.

The availability of proper materials would be the second necessity in pottery development. An exception to this rule, though, was discovered by the University of Oregon group supervised by David Cole. They found pottery dishes in the Klamath River Canyon of Oregon, where there is no nearby source of pottery material.

Baked clay objects (Fig. 140) are normally not considered as pottery, but they do indicate that pottery techniques were known to some extent. Such pieces, though rare, are occasionally found in Oregon. No. 4 is a fragment of a poorly made clay pipe. No. 3 shows round, baked marbles of clay or mud. The purpose of these balls is unknown; possibly they were for a game. The highly decorated object in No. 2 appears to have had a string molded in the wet clay and then withdrawn in order to leave a hole. It could be a fragment of pipe but it resembles a snake pattern more than anything else. The disk at the top of the picture (No. 1) is thought to be a clay bead (for lack of any other explanation of its purpose).

Dr. Leroy Johnson of the University of Oregon was asked to examine the piece; he said it was identical to the spindle whorls he had found in Mexico while conducting research there. These whorls are used on primitive spindles to aid in the manipulation of the thread when spinning. This unusual disk is found again in Fig. 141, between a decorated spindle whorl (left) from Mexico and two pottery spinning devices from the Hohokam culture of

Fig. 140. Baked clay pieces.

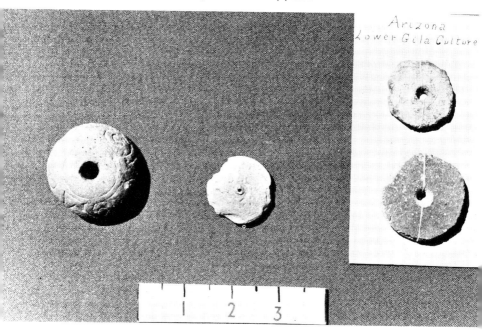

Arizona
Lower Gila Culture

Fig. 141. Comparison of artifacts from Mexico, Clear Lake, and Arizona.

Arizona. Similar clay objects are also found in central California. The clay objects could have been traded in from Mexico or from other Indians who had the skill to work in ceramics. Trading from such a distance seems almost inconceivable, yet it is entirely possible that this small clay wheel came from there. This find strengthens the evidence that the three-legged mortar mentioned in Chapter 4 was traded from Mexico.

Wall of China

Carr Butte is the name of the round-shaped mountain lying between Langell Valley and Clear Lake. It honors the Carr family, who purchased the ranch from Jesse Applegate on the northwest shore of the lake. A sign just south of Carr Butte used to point to a dim road labeled Fiddler's Green, but the sign is no longer there; it has been replaced by a forest road number. The legend of Fiddler's Green is still strong in the minds of many of the old-timers who herded sheep or cattle near the early Carr Ranch headquarters. Also still evident are the remains of the Wall of China, built in the late 1870s and early 1880s by the Chinese laborers brought from San Francisco. The native basalt rocks were piled into a fence to confine the cattle herds and to hold out those owned by the homesteaders of Langell Valley.

At times of low water, springs and land appear where the old Carr buildings stood. Here, the bullets, horseshoes, and meat hooks of the historic West are mingled with the mortars, obsidian points, and pestles of those prehistoric occupants who used the springs before the white men came. It was near here that the blonde ghost with the long hair and the violin made the Green a poor place for Irish sheepherders and passing cowboys to spend the night.

Legend of Fiddler's Green

There are several versions of the story of the ghost of Fiddler's Green. The fact that the lonely cabin still stands there by the large spring makes the story all the more believable. No human being lives near the many miles of the lake shore, and the solitude alone is enough to cause even the skeptical to give credence to the legend.

According to one version, a homesteader completed his house near the Applegate Trail and then decided to send east for a mail-order bride. When she arrived, he was overjoyed, for she was not only beautiful, but she was also a talented violinist. A short time after their marriage, she was murdered by robbers who chanced to pass along the wagon road in front of the homestead. They threw the body into the spring, where it was discovered by the grieving husband.

The ghost of the bride, its blonde hair falling below its shoulders, is said to emerge at night from the spring to play the violin. Several sightings of the ethereal visitor have been reported. Ben Murphy of Klamath Falls told me of one such appearance. His father, Dan Murphy, grazed sheep in the region of Clear Lake over a period of years, and Ben's boyhood summers were spent with some of the herders. On one occasion, two of the herders had camped at Fiddler's Green with their flock bedded close by. One went to the spring for water and upon his return to the tent was accompanied by the ghost. His partner decided the only reasonable course to follow was immediate departure. This decision was quickly acted upon by the Irish boy without so much as a good-by to his companion. Several miles later, the shepherd arrived at Malin, breathless and exhausted.

Hoping to find some solid basis for this story, I asked my friend Ben if the story was told to him in all seriousness. He replied: "Who can tell when an Irishman is serious, or seriously lying?" In any case, I never see the cabin without thinking of the legend, and never see the Wall of China nearby, without picturing the Chinese as they lifted the rocks into place to build the fence.

Sweat Baths

The bare beaches of Clear Lake reveal another type of structure abandoned considerably before the Applegates made the southern route of the Oregon Trail along its shores. These structures are made of stone and range in width from four to twenty feet. They consist only of rocks grouped closely together as though to form a masonry floor. The large number of the structures strengthens the theory that the area was occupied for centuries. An occasional stone implement, usually broken, occurs on some of them. One theory is that they were used for roasting food. The most common belief is that they were sweat baths. The steam for a sweat bath was provided by pouring water on heated rocks inside an enclosure. Tule mats were placed around the sweat houses to contain the heat. The Klamath Indians reported that three such permanent structures were on the Upper Klamath Lake. One large stone structure over thirty feet across still exists near Algoma.

Both the cleanliness and spiritual needs of the bather were served by the sweat bath. It was a place of purification following a death in a family, and a place of preparation for an important event such as a hunt, gambling, or a raid. Illness was cured, or made worse, by this form of treatment. Charles Drew, who bought cattle from the Indians, reported that many of the Indian families living near Sprague River maintained a mat-covered sweat bath in their back yards even after moving into government-built houses.

Pelican Islands

From the north shore of Clear Lake it is possible to observe several low islands in the distance. In late spring the islands are marked with large white patches: the flocks of nesting white pelicans with their awkward progeny. These strange birds must have discovered and used the nesting islands long before man migrated to North America, and they continue to use them today even though the artificially controlled level of the lake fluctuates greatly. The islands provide refuge from coyotes and other killers, and currently they provide protection from man through the services of the U. S. Fish and Wildlife Service. Pelicans, with their strong flocking instinct, both fly and fish in formation. In summer they can be detected at great heights by the flash of the sun on their wings—and they are said to be the only bird that flies for pleasure. In their food-gathering activities, they may congregate on any lake or stream which contains fish. Even in the city limits of Klamath Falls on Link River, a few pelicans can usually be observed.

Their group activity in fishing is fascinating. They will form a half circle, gliding along on the water with seemingly motionless feet, like some Russian dancers whose coats disguise the movement of their feet. The hungry birds then close in on the fish, losing their dignity when they lift their long beaks into the air to allow gravity to drop the flopping fish victims into their gullets. Once they are full, the adult birds return to their coyote-proof nesting place to regurgitate the contents of their gullets for the offspring. Flying or swimming, a pelican is a graceful sight; but a walking pelican is comic, and a dining pelican is awkward.

It was their slow footwork that made the partly grown birds a natural resource of considerable interest to the primitive "bird lovers" of Clear Lake. An event of exceptional rarity was witnessed at Clear Lake in the 1880s by Jim Dixon, an early-day cowboy who later settled at Klamath Falls. Dixon was riding for cattle in the area when he came upon a small band of Indians reported as Klamaths. (It is believed, however, that they were Modocs from Yainax, who had formerly been residents of the Clear Lake area.) The band had made their encampment and built willow-pole racks. Then they killed the nearly grown pelicans with clubs, dressed the birds, and dried them on the racks in the sun. In this way the birds were preserved and carried back to the reservation to be used for winter food.

Bone Implements

The bones of the pelicans, like those of other water birds, served the ancient Indians as material for the making of their tools, beads, and pipe stems, long after the edible portions of the birds had been consumed. In addition to using bird bones for pipe stems, they also used them for making piercing awls such as those pictured directly above the measuring marker in Fig. 142. All other items in this figure are made from the bones of mammals. The three flat pieces in the upper center have some decoration and are thought to be hair ornaments. Parts of them are still quite shiny from long use. The longest round bones (on either side of the horizontal center specimens) resemble the fossil projectile points found on Lower Klamath Lake and at Kawumkan Springs. The lack of beveling suggests that they might have served some other purpose, perhaps that of a hairpin.

The round-ended mammal bone on the lower right in Fig. 142 is shaped in a manner to allow its use as a spoon. The remaining bones can be classified as bone awls, although they vary greatly in shape and workmanship. Some are simply bone splinters with one sharpened end. Without doubt, the utility of these crude punches is as great as the others which have been shaped and even ornamented. The smallest awl on the dark paper is the small bone from the side of a deer's lower leg.

The Ipo People

It has been mentioned that a great diversity of stone objects in the Lost River Circle could have been caused by the tremendous time span in the period of occupation, or by the numerous neighbors who lived on the frontiers of these people. A third explanation for the diversity might be the differences in types of food available and used during the period of occupation.

The studies of archeologists have established that the development of many Klamath stone implements resulted from improving the processing of wocas. It seems certain to the writer that many of the varied stones in the Clear Lake region are the tools used in the processing of a small native plant-root called the ipo. In the original language of the Lutuami (lake people), these tubers were called kas kash. Gatschet said that the word

Fig. 142. Bone pieces were usually undecorated.

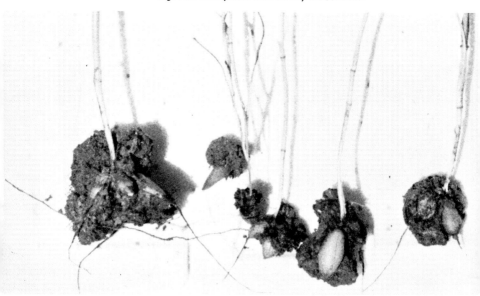

Fig. 143. Ipo bulb clusters.

ipo was a Shasta term, later adopted by the Klamaths who called it apaw.

In *Wild Flowers of the Pacific Coast*, Leslie Haskin confirms Gatschet's statement by saying: "The Klamath name of ipo, epo, or apo (variously spelled) for *Carum oreganum*, is an adaptation from more southern tribes, and is possibly a corruption of the Spanish word *apio*, celery." In describing the roots he added: "I have often gathered these roots and eaten them, and at present am growing them in my garden. When baked they burst open, exposing the dry mealy interior, and are very appetizing. They are also extremely good when fried in butter. Squirrels are fond of these roots, and in the Cascade Mountains gather large amounts of them for their winter stores."

The ipo is quite widely dispersed in the Northwest, and grows somewhat larger when rainfall is more ample. Fig. 143 gives an idea of the shape of the bulb clusters found around Clear Lake.

These tubers were dug by many Indian tribes in the North-west. Lewis and Clark said the Shoshones called them year-pah and made this observation on their quality: "These roots are very palatable either fresh, roasted, boiled, or dried, and are generally between the size of a quill and a man's finger, and about the length of the latter [much longer than those at Clear Lake] . . . The body or consistence of the root is white, mealy, and easily reduced by pounding to a substance resembling flour, which thickens with boiling water like flour, and is agreeably flavored." They noted the flavor was not unlike anise seed.

The white bloom of the ipo is easy to identify as it resembles a wild parsnip or carrot bloom in shape and grows on a virtually leafless stem. The species growing in the Modoc country seems to have made an extremely delicate adjustment to moisture conditions. One area may be covered with the plants, while an adjacent rock flat has none. Despite this seemingly narrow range of habitat, there are actually thousands of acres on the flats surrounding Clear Lake that are still ornamented by the blooms of the ipo during the summer (Fig. 144).

The effect of this fine food resource upon the many generations of "hunting and gathering" people is not hard to imagine. Erin Forrest, a Pit River Indian who spent much of his childhood on the rock flats southeast of Clear Lake, said the ipo was one of the principal items of diet. The small tubers always seem to choose a rocky environment and grow nearly six inches under the surface. Harvesting them with a stick required considerable effort; yet this was only the first step in preparing them for eventual consumption. Erin Forrest said that his people readied them for storage in two ways: the first method was to break the bulbs up in a mortar, then shape them by hand into balls for drying and for future use; the second method was to dry them for storage, then grind them into a flour on a metate.

Ipo Preparation Required Many Stones

Such processing techniques might well require three or more different milling devices for the final product. The presence of the surprising number of mortars and metates on one site suggests a double processing of the same food. (It should be noted that there is a lack of stratification since the stones here are simply covered by the elements. Conceivably they became intermingled by the ice erosion.) Certainly the acres of ipos on the miles of scab-rock flats surrounding the area could supply the raw material for a large milling industry. The suggested possibility that the many mortars were the result of an acorn culture during the past climatic cycles seems so remote in this juniper-sagebrush ecology that it should be dismissed unless substantial proof is offered.

Mortars which were common around Tule Lake and Clear Lake up to a few years ago are shown in Fig. 145. These are called "Lazy-Wife" mortars by the writer because they seem to lack any general shape and do not exhibit the workmanship capability that the women used in the early cultures. The wander-

Fig. 144. Ipo plant blooms on the Applegate Trail near Clear Lake. (DeVere photo)

Fig.145. Lazy-wife mortar and mortar ground into a basalt column.

ing people on the deserts east of Burns, Oregon, left such simple grinders in their temporary campsites—probably because a heavy mortar was difficult to transport and much too valuable to leave at each camping place. These indented rocks are an adaptation of the bedrock type to a smaller stone. A basketry hopper was probably used on the stone pictured at the left. This served as a substitute for the upper portion of the rim of the bowl. The bowl at the right was made by taking a lava basalt column and making a hole in it without shaping the exterior.

Making Stone Tools

When the difficulty of manufacturing mortars and other stone-age objects is considered, it is a wonder that so many were well finished. The press of other matters in the process of making a living would undoubtedly limit the time available for shaping stone pieces, which must have been a slow and laborious process.

Clifford and Mike Clayton of Klamath Falls found two stone pieces in Modoc County which clearly illustrate the methods used in bringing the stone into its final form. Fig. 146 shows (at left) a mortar which has been put to some use, but the owner was still apparently in the process of pecking off a knob which protrudes from one side. The stone on the right has been worn down to a diameter that enabled the maker to break it away from the parent stone.

For this process of shaping and pecking stone implements into form, other stones were used. They can sometimes be distinguished as hammer stones such as those in Fig. 147. The stone at the left has a crystalline structure with signs of wear on each end. The one on the right has been provided with indentations for the thumb of the user.

Basalt Tools

The debris remaining from a stone-age Indian camp usually contains many broken pestles and cooking rocks of irregular shape, along with reject obsidian. Among these waste materials

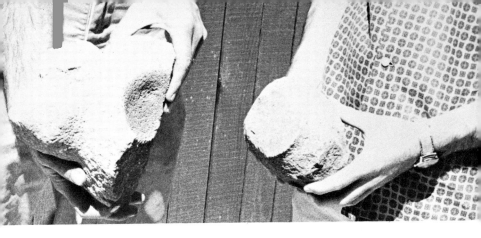

Fig. 146. Stones were shaped by pecking and hammering.

Fig. 147. Hard rocks were selected for hammer stones.

a more dense type of stone is usually present. These hard nodules do not look like tools and are not prized by collectors or museums. Close examination reveals that while they have not been shaped, they are chipped from use in fashioning other stone objects. They were doubtless of greater utility to the artisans who used them than many of the more shapely artifacts.

Another group of tools, which were undoubtedly much more prized by their makers than by those who collect them, were the basalt scrapers, called "cobble choppers" by Emory Strong in his *Stone Age on the Columbia River*. Those in Fig. 148 are the type found at Clear Lake. These are generally larger than those occurring on other sites of the Klamath highland. The exact use cannot be determined, but judging from the numbers, they must have been very popular. Cracking bones, scraping hides or wood, and shaping other stones are all possibilities for their use.

Fig. 149 shows a basalt tool from Warner Valley which has been converted into a very effective stone saw. The angle of the flake has made a cutting edge on both sides of the "blade." The insert on the figure shows a small obsidian tool believed to have been used for a saw.

The Mortar in Food Preparation

The more ancient occupants of the Lost River Circle produced a better mortar than the "Lazy-Wife" type, although the coarse-grained stone was not conducive to the manufacture of the smooth, highly finished mortars such as those found along the Columbia or Willamette rivers. Fig. 150 shows a series of five Clear Lake mortars. The flat-bottomed type was favored here, although the small one at the right has a pointed bottom. The two on either side of the center were found cached side by side, upside down, as though the owner had gone on a trip expecting to return and recover them. One contained an ordinary double-ended pestle like that inside the pointed mortar at the right. This pestle was found in place, imbedded in the mineralized dirt, and has never been removed.

Fig. 148. Flaked basalt choppers were useful tools.

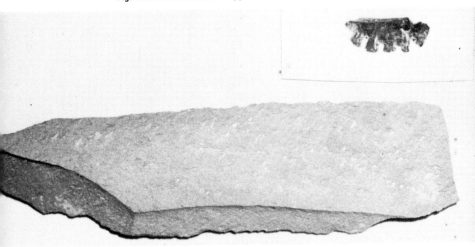

Fig. 149. The large basalt saw had two cutting edges. The insert, a small obsidian tool, was believed to have been used as a saw.

Fig. 150. (below) The double-ended pestle was preferred in the Lost River Circle.

The pointed-bottom mortars were shaped in this fashion for insertion in the soil. This gave greater stability for the circular grinding motion of the pestle. The inside bottoms of the holes in the stone vessels are nearly conical in shape, except in the smaller paint-pot types. This contrasts with the round-bottom shape of the Calapooia mortars shown in Fig. 151, which appear to have been used for pounding food instead of grinding it. The two on the outside are Calapooia mortars; the center one is from Clear Lake.

The handy corner grocery store and the supermarket have made the thought of a food shortage seem so remote to modern man that it is virtually impossible for him to realize the difficulty of survival for even the most fortunate Indians. They had to find, catch, or kill food; then grind, pound, or cook it to the point where it could be chewed. Preparation of food by grinding in stone vessels and cooking with hot rocks was an extremely slow process. Chewing of the food was itself a major problem. Mrs. O. T. Anderson, Sr., a long-time resident of Beatty, Oregon, related how her mother, "who had lived in the old ways," described the difficulty of simply chewing the things necessary to get enough to eat. It was a tiresome and often an all-day job to eat the only food that could be found at certain seasons of the year.

One way that the older Indians compensated for their particular chewing problems was by giving the food additional grinding in a small mortar. Some call these small mortars paint pots; others call them old people's mortars. In Fig. 152, the small mortar on the left from Warner Valley was probably a paint-grinding bowl since it is too small to have utility for food. The three on the right from the Lost River Circle could well be old people's mortars, used to give relief to the worn-down teeth, or gums from which the teeth had departed.

The mortar shown in the center of Fig. 153 exceeds 140 pounds in weight and is over 19 inches in height. The pointed bottom on this mortar from Lower Klamath Lake indicates again the difference from the type prepared by the Clear Lake resi-

Fig. 151. The Calapooia mortars were much flatter in comparison with the common Clear Lake type.

Fig. 152. Old people's mortars.

Fig. 153. (below) Giant pointed mortar flanked by the flat-bottom types.

dents. Old pictures indicate that these enormous bowls were used with only two or three inches of the rim extending above the soil in which they were buried. Long double-ended pestles were normally employed, although the one pictured here has a knob on the end.

Metates

If the Klamaths exhibited the best inventive genius in the development of the mano, certainly the Lost River Circle people manifest the greatest ingenuity in the variety of metates that were produced. Fig. 154 shows three metates of the oval type; the one on the left has a slight rim. The three manos in the upper part of the picture all have a slight depression worked into the top as though for additional use as either an anvil or a bowl.

The most common type of metate is the flat stone, poorly worked but showing wear on one or both sides. The Clear Lake people made and used more types of metates than any other tribes, with the possible exception of the Indians of Mexico. Some were square-shaped and had a perfectly flat grinding surface like those in Fig. 155. Manos found with these usually exhibit a plane surface as contrasted with a more curving surface of others. A third type of large metate found is triangular in shape, perhaps to be held on the lap. The metate on the left in Fig. 156 has a raised lip on the lower side, perhaps for better containment of the materials being ground. Evidence indicates, however, that a mat was often placed under the metate to prevent loss of the precious contents.

The "bathtub metates" shown in Fig. 157 are among the most prized collector's items to be found, and most of them in this region have been found in the Lost River Circle. All are elongated with raised edges and usually have one open end for working the foodstuff out onto the mat. The sides of the "bathtub" are not nearly so high as the corn-country metates of Arizona and Mexico, but they are a distinct type. The one at the left in Fig. 157 has been sharpened by having grooves incised in

Fig. 154. Size of oval-shaped metates is shown by the one-foot ruler.

Fig. 155. Some rectangular metates were found with large flat manos.

Fig. 156. Triangular-shaped stones.

Fig. 157. Bathtub-shaped metates were sometimes sharpened like a millstone.

the stone like the grooves in a millstone. This sharpening is also found on other types of metates although not so frequently as upon the bathtub type. The underside of the one pictured second from the left is so round that it was thought to be a partly buried pestle when found upside down. The handsome "bathtub metate" in Fig. 158, from the Ramona and Bill Carter Collection, was found together with the unique single-knob mano pictured. The grain in the metate is wocas.

Antelope Country

The pronghorn antelope is presently numerous enough in the Clear Lake country to permit hunting them—of course outside the extensive boundaries of the wildlife refuge. This graceful animal undoubtedly served as a protein supplement in the diet of the Modocs and their Pit River neighbors. One method used in hunting the antelope was to station hunters along the route and then conduct drives. A second method was to exploit the curiosity of these animals. Though they are fleet footed and very timid, antelope are extremely curious and can at times be lured near a hunter if he simply remains motionless or gently waves a cloth on the end of a stick.

During the mating season in August, the males change completely in personality and—with their harems of does gathered about them—become as dictatorial as an oriental despot. The points of land jutting into Clear Lake provide ideal places for the does to be kept separate.

A vigorous buck has a dual problem. He must fend off the other bucks and he must hook and crowd the does into a compact group to keep them from straying. Besides, there always seems to be the additional problem of a few of the very young and the very old making a nuisance of themselves around the edge of his area. The present writer believes that, to the does, the sagebrush always looks greener on the other side of the ridge. A second—and uncalled for—observation of the writer is that, over the centuries, the female of Homo sapiens has gained sufficient control over her society to enforce a legal system requiring monogamy.

Gaming Stones

A group of people may achieve an identifying trademark through the development of a specialized tool such as the Klamaths' two-horned mano. They may also acquire a name or trademark through the manufacture of great numbers of a given product, such as the Calapooias with their quantities of tiny, triangular, serrated arrowpoints.

The Lost River Circle people probably should be identified with a small football-shaped artifact called a gaming stone by archeologists. The reason for calling them gaming stones is the theory that because of their convenient size and shape—like an elongated lemon—they were hidden in the hand for a guessing game similar to the stick game.

There is much evidence that they had some other purpose also. Their great abundance along the entire course of Lost River and around Clear Lake would indicate an appetite for gambling far exceeding anything ever seen in Las Vegas. Fig. 159 shows some of these stones in the back yard of the writer. Further evidence that they were used for some purpose other than gaming is that they were often found in a group. Up to thirty-two in a group have been reported. Some of these were so crudely shaped as to be unrecognizable if not associated with others of this type. A third piece of evidence supporting some other use is the location of the "finds"—which is almost always near the edge of a river or lake. The writer personally believes that they were weights for a casting net similar to the one Hawaiian fishermen use. The capture of ducks or fish might have been the purpose of the nets.

Dr. Arnold Shotwell, a paleontologist and head of the University of Oregon Museum of Natural History, has little sympathy for the puzzled archeologist. When a problem of identifying a given stone is brought to him, he has a ready-made answer which provides little relief to the archeologist, but affords some pleasure to the paleontologist. His explanation of these stones is that they were "dog rocks," which he says were made to throw at undisciplined dogs lurking about the campfires.

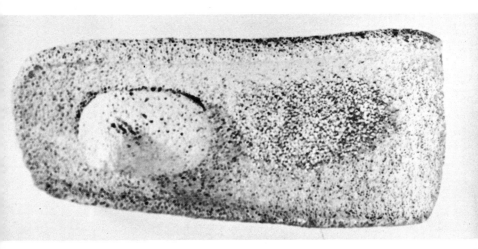

Fig. 158. Bathtub metate found with a single horned mano.

Fig. 159. Gaming stones, net weights, or dog rocks?

The deep canyon of the Klamath River provided a rough but passable trade route through the Cascade Mountains. This pass near the California-Oregon border enabled the Modocs of the Lower Klamath region to carry on commerce with coastal tribes.

6. THE RICH TRADERS OF LOWER KLAMATH LAKE

Trade Goods of the Modocs

The narrows in the Columbia River at Wishram illustrate how a geological feature can affect the activities of man. Here an Indian trading community was created by natural river-route features which funneled traders through a narrow passage, causing them briefly to change their method of transportation from boat to portage.

The entrance to the Klamath River Canyon must have had a similar effect upon the Modocs who lived nearby on Lower Klamath Lake, though this proximity to the travel route toward the California Coast would not by itself have brought trade. The Modocs also had to have commodities desired by the Shastas, Yuroks, Karoks, and others who lived along the lower river. These goods took many forms: obsidian from Glass Mountain, wocas seeds, dried camas and dried mushrooms, elk-horn implements and elk-skin armor, and the dried flesh of waterfowl, mullet, and salmon. Perhaps some of these goods were packed in the waterproof tule cooking baskets made by the nimble fingers of the Modoc maidens.

Pit River slaves and feather blankets also added to the expendable wealth of these fortunate ones; small wonder that they so fiercely defended their productive homeland. It is also easy to understand why their population grew and prospered; but why the numbers of these rich traders later dwindled is hard to understand.

Lower Klamath Lake

One of the greatest unsolved mysteries of Lower Klamath Lake is the fact that so few Indians lived there at the time of the coming of the white man, when the basin supported such a large population in earlier times. The story of the decline of these people might not have come to light if the entire surface of the broad lake basin had not been devastated by erosion. The great, flat expanse presented a scene of almost complete desolation during the dry years of the 1930s. On windy days, even the rabbits hardly dared open their eyes in the dust. On calm days, the heat waves caused a mirage effect that made the volcanic islands appear higher and closer than they actually were. Tall "dust devils" created by whirlwinds seemed to stand motionless in these vast, lonely stretches.

The key to the mystery of these people seems to lie in the structure of the lake basin itself. If the Creator had set out to engineer a basin to regulate the flow of the Klamath River, it could not have been done much better than it was with the creation of Lower Klamath Lake.

When the river was high in the spring runoff period, the water flowed through the natural strait and into the lake. On one occasion, a former steamboat captain on the river, the late Judge U. E. Reeder, said that if he could get the *Canby*, a paddle-wheel steamer, into this strait by evening they could go to sleep. By morning, the inflowing waters would have carried the boat through the strait into the open lake. From there a choice of fresh-water docks was available: the Chalk Bank to unload lumber for Merrill, Laird's Landing for freight, or Oklahoma Landing to pick up a load of hay.

In the fall of the year, as the river lowered, the flow would be reversed and the stream would come from the lake, thus maintaining the level of the river. It was this marriage of the lake and the river that caused Peter Skene Ogden and other early-day travelers to veer to the east and through the crossroads at Tule Lake. An impassable marsh existed for several miles from Midland to the volcanic island at Ady. Only a canoe, and later the steamboat, could penetrate this region.

Modoc Villages

One village, Stuikishxeni (meaning "at the canoe bay"), was located near Midland on the lake's edge. This camp existed into the historic period along with a few others; Gatschet's informants told him of five permanent villages on Lower Klamath Lake.

This sparsity of Indian population on Lower Klamath at the coming of the white man is also borne out by the lack of trade goods—such as glass beads and metal objects—in the camping places of the Lower Klamath Modocs. This is in contrast to their Klamath neighbors who left an unbroken chain of trade goods from the frontier with the Modocs on the Klamath River, clear to the most northern outposts at Klamath Marsh.

Even though the Lower Lake Modocs were small in numbers at the time of white contact, the shores of this lake have proved to be an almost continuous archeological site. A site thousands of years old has even been found in the center of the lake at one of the deepest places. Nevertheless, the revelation of the materials and habits of these people had to await the works of modern man who unintentionally uncovered the secrets. A railroad from the south was pushed to Ady, then on north—cutting off the steamboat passage at the strait—and then into the city of Klamath Falls.

The lands of the marsh adjacent to the "Canoe Bay" were diked for agricultural purposes. This served to remove the major source of water for the lake, since the waters of the creeks, which had entered the lake from the south end, had long before been utilized for irrigation. With the water gone, the tules and other plants of the wide, flat basin were unable to survive the arid weather cycle which occurred in the 1930s. After the plants died, the cutting power of the wind soon removed the cover and scoured into the black humus of the lake bottom (Fig. 160). Even though they were twenty miles away, the billowing clouds of dust gave the housewives of Klamath Falls cause to complain. Dusk would sometimes come in the middle of the day as a result of these windstorms.

Erosion Reveals Remains of Ancient Man

The exciting possessions of the lake dwellers were soon exposed, slowly at first; but as the dryness increased, the erosive processes ate into the homesites and even into the graves around the lake. When the water lowered, the continuing pressure of the wind removed the muck from the lake bottom. After the muck was gone, a layer of pumice blew off, exposing a layer of white hardpan. On the hardpan were found chipped objects in association with bluish-colored fossil bones. These, together with a punch-like object of fossilized bone and a stone-pipe fragment, were given to the University of Oregon for examination. The fossil bones proved to be those of a camel, and the bone punch was identified as a projectile point.

It has been estimated that the age of these people dates back some six thousand or more years. Their artifacts include not only chipped objects, but all the stone objects normally found in a village site.

The strange presence of this village on one of the deepest parts of the lake can be explained either of two ways. There could have been an exceedingly dry period, during which time the lake might have been so low that animals grazed on the edge of a stream or marsh and man camped there. Or, there could have been a shift in the rock fault at Keno, which controls the level of the river just before it plunges into the canyon. In support of the latter theory, John C. Cleghorn, a consulting engineer

Fig. 160. Dry winds removed the soil cover from the Indian camps.

Fig. 161. The bolas were used to entangle the legs of birds or animals.

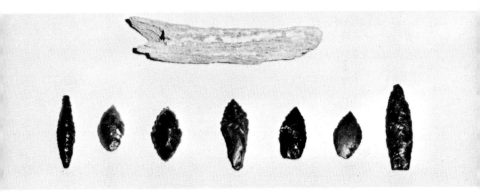

Fig. 162. The fossil camel rib may belong with the projectile points.

of Klamath Falls, conducted studies which indicate that the levels of both the Lower Klamath Lake and Tule Lake basins would be subject to the shifting of this fault. However, the dry cycle theory seems more logical in view of the world-wide drought which occurred at about the age fixed for the existence of this culture.

The bola stones (Fig. 161) were found at this low level. These stones, attached to the ends of a thong or cord, were used for hurling and entangling birds or small mammals. The attachment is through a hole bored in one end rather than by means of a notched girdle like those found on the ancient Columbia River sites. A third ball is sometimes attached to a cord about half the length of the main cord at a point bisecting the latter. Bolas, a word of Spanish origin, were certainly not unique with these local Indians, having been used in areas as remote as South America and the Aleutian Islands.

A few chipped objects found in the old sites, together with a fragment of camel rib, are shown in Fig. 162. There is, of course, a decided difference between these and the later arrowpoints of the Modocs.

Island Gave Protection

During the centuries that man lived on the Lower Klamath, he seems to have been drawn to the islands which existed during the various levels of the water. Frank Payne, a collector from Klamath Falls, discovered some of these island villages and made careful observations of them on his many trips to the site. These records are preserved, together with the specimens he collected, in the Klamath County Museum. The attractiveness of the islands as a place to live could be discovered only after the surface blew off.

It may seem strange to the present-day observer that these lake-dwellers would accept the inconvenience of communication with the mainland in order to receive the protection the islands offered, but an entry in Peter Skene Ogden's Journals offers a good explanation of the need for protection. On Jauary 23, 1827, he wrote: "In this spot formerly a Tribe of Indians resided that have all been destroyed by the Clammett Nation. Not one now remains—about a dozen families who had endeavored to save themselves by flight but in vain and every soul murdered." The "Clammett" mentioned by Ogden were more likely to have been Modocs than Klamaths, who (according to Frain who was born in the Klamath Canyon) were the group making occasional excursions into Shasta country. Such intertribal attacks may also account for the small numbers existent at the time of white contact.

Names and Songs

Indian place names, like the names of people, were given with a descriptive quality. Chewaucan is a corruption of the Lutuami word Tchuaxeni, "where the arrow leaf (wapato) is found." Another, "Kawamxani, "the eel spring," is listed by Gatschet. From evidence available, the names of people were often not complimentary. Dried Leg, Left-Handed, Two Rumps Having, Grizzlies' Nose, and Big Belly are actual examples of Indian names and provide clues to the techniques used in giving them. A principal brave of the Modoc War was named Scarface Charley, a descriptive name that was the aftermath of a childhood accident.

The frankness used in bestowing names carried over into the songs. The old expression, "You can get it for a song," had real meaning during the centuries when the Modoc people swarmed about the islands and shores of Klamath Lake; like the stories, the songs were used for many purposes. There were songs of satire, which when translated from the Lutuami dialect still seem humorous: "He goes around giving away sticks of tobacco and is very noisy about it." Another song, "Slow running horses he paid for his wife," might cease to be humorous after being repeated in a metered style of the Modocs for a period of time.

The dullness of the food-gathering work was evidently relieved by rhythmic singing with such words as: "The young girl shakes her body when planting the camas stick in the ground."

Indian love songs, quite different from those currently played upon the violin, were in vogue. The following one, for group singing, had separate parts for boys and girls—Girls: "Young man, I will not love you for you run around with no blanket on; I do not desire such a husband." Boys: "And I do not like a frog-shaped woman with swollen eyes." However, not all songs dealing with the sexes showed such a lack of tenderness.

The war songs were often a combination of syllables, having tune and rhythm without any particular meaning; but it was the songs for the treatment of the sick that provided the greatest expression for the individuality of the composer, who was also the owner of the song.

Shaman Doctors

The healing art, as practiced by the lake people, was frequently an audience-participation event, for the songs of the shaman often required a chorus. "Doctor" is not a satisfactory name for the healers of either the Modoc or the Klamath tribes, for they rarely administered medicine to their patients. The title of shaman—or "conjurer" as Gatschet refers to them—more adequately describes their work. Many of them were women, some of whom built reputations as specialists for healing certain diseases.

It took considerable effort to become a shaman and often involved no small risk. Three things were necessary. First was a vision. The power quest was a mission common to most ordinary members of a village; but a vision, more powerful and severe than ordinary—occasionally accompanied by fasting, loss of consciousness, and blood running from the mouth—was a requisite of the shaman's internship. In addition to a vision which brought power, the shaman also had to have a song. The song repeated over and over in a monotonous voice was as much a part of the healer's stock-in-trade as a fever thermometer is today. A third need was the curing tool, in which form the power of the vision

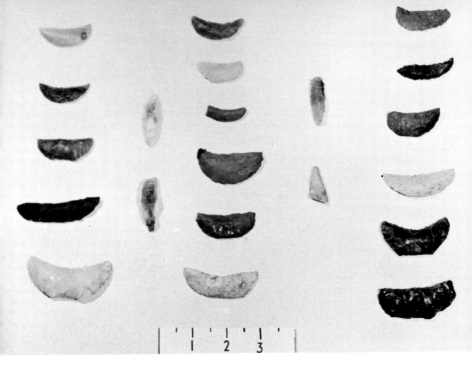

Fig. 163. The makers of crescents such as these usually selected colored stone.

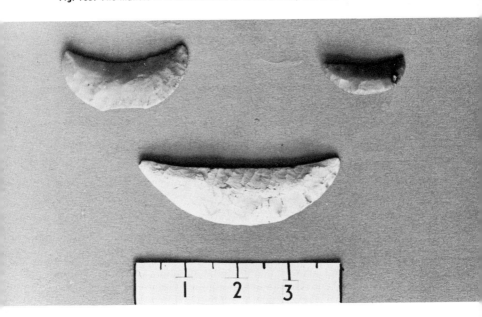

Fig. 164. The stone-age people of Denmark used a crescent larger than those made locally.

was often expressed. Sometimes the shaman sucked upon the affected part and pretended to bring out the disease.

Stephen Powers, in his study for the Bureau of American Ethnology, after observing practices of the shaman in Northern California, said that a frog or fish might be vomited up as a manifestation of the removal of the disease. The crescent-shaped stones (Fig. 163) are thought by Hugh Worcester, former Fish and Wildlife official, to have been objects used by conjurers in a manner similar to that described by Powers. He thought the crescent was hidden in the hand or mouth, and then either pulled from the mouth of the shaman or from some part of the ill person's body. Exhibits in the Indian Museum at Sacramento, California, confirm Worcester's theory. These crescents are quite rare and are usually made of colored stone. A camp near Christmas Lake, christened "Shaman's Camp" by collectors, produced several of these stones, along with some unusual chipped agates. Colored crescents have also been found in limited numbers at the other sites mentioned in this book.

A white crescent from the stone age in Denmark is shown in the lower part of Fig. 164. Above it are two more crescents— found at Silver Lake (left) and at Lower Klamath Lake (right). The flint piece from Denmark is about twice or three times as large as most local crescents, but otherwise it is much the same. Some collectors have called these pieces "moon stones," "worship stones," or "fish scrapers." They may have also been used as ornaments; but lacking further evidence, the explanation that they were a part of the conjurer's instrument kit seems as good as any.

The song and the healing object were usually used together. Often the neighbors were called into "the sing" to join the chorus. During the ceremony, conjurers exerted great effort, sucking, blowing on whistles, dancing, and gesticulating. In addition to the crescent, other objects of "medicine" were frequently used. One healing man recorded by Gatschet pretended to pull a rope

from his mouth. His song was: "Kenuks a-I Nu Stu Nxi Uapk"—
"I will pull a rope from my entrails."

The shaman could even get the help of animals as he brand-
ished his magic instruments and sang:

So looks the medicine tool taken from the yellow hammer.
This is my curing tool that of the otter.
This is my curing tool that of the otter skin belt.

He could also make mysterious symbols on the house floor
and on the body of the diseased: "Lu Pakh Ge-U Muluash"—
"White chalk is my curing tool." And one medicine song indicated that the bone paddle was used for the extraction of disease.

Another example of the curing tools of the shaman is shown
in Fig. 165. This set of bone whistles was found on the Klamath
River near Keno by Leroy Gienger. Beautifully carved, they differ from the type used as game-calls as they are larger and have
had great effort expended on them. The game-calls may be a
simple bird or mammal bone with a hole cut in one side.

A set of two shaman's whistles was found near Barclay Springs
by Bill Foster and Bob Anderson of Klamath Falls. The maker
did a beautiful job of carving, but for some reason he made the
top and bottom of each whistle according to a different design
(Fig. 166). The topside of the shorter whistle has four finger
holes and could therefore be called a flute. Note its different underside design in the lower photo. The longer whistle shows the
same bone tube turned upside down.

Certainly not all bone whistles were used by conjurers, nor
can it be said positively that any given one was used by a doctor.
The Indians throughout North America used game-calls of varied
types. Charles Preuss, the German cartographer who made maps
for John C. Fremont, mentions that one of Fremont's men traded
a bone game-call from an Indian at about the same time they
first came through the Blue Moutains of Eastern Oregon. The
simple whistles shown in Fig. 167 from Lower Klamath Lake are
believed to have been used for game-calls.

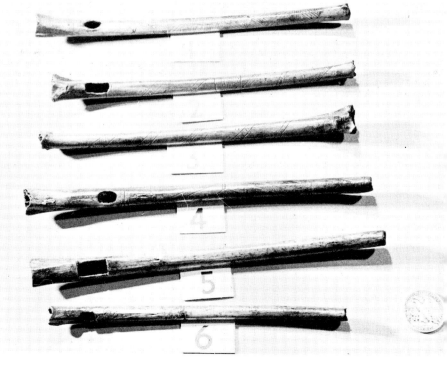

Fig. 165. Decorated whistles found together.

Fig. 166. Both sides of two "whistles." The shorter one has several finger holes like a flute. Note the different pattern on the reverse side.

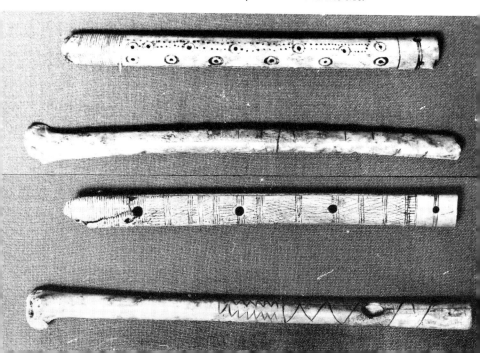

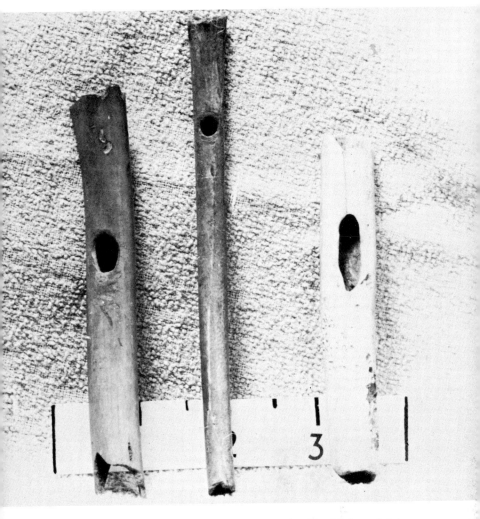

Fig. 167. Whistles used for game calls were much simpler. (Van Landrum photo)

The writer tried without success for a number of years to make a noise that even remotely resembled animal, fish, or fowl, by blowing on one of these alleged bone game-calls. Quite by chance, a man living in the Sierra Madre Mountains of Mexico demonstrated how wild turkeys can be called by using a bone tube. Since that time, it is easy to see how ducks, geese, even coyotes and deer, could be attracted by using such a device. A hunter with an empty stomach to encourage him should be able to develop real artistry.

Another strange and unusual find (Fig. 168) shows part of a cache of over fifty heron heads. These were found by Mrs. Gienger on the O'Connor Ranch at the north shore of the lake. They are thought to be from a shaman's cloak or belt and were probably part of the colorful ritual which accompanied the treatment of patients.

One can almost imagine the quandary of the ancient practitioners: Should the power of the weasel be called? Should the north wind be solicited? Or, was this a job for the spider medicine? One would indeed need to be very sick not to respond to the dancing, chanting, and tooting which were interspersed with the hypnotic answers of the chorus, standing by to back up the incantations of the chief surgeon. The power of the watersnake could be called forth. Frog, marten, and crane were also summoned—according to the songs of the conjurers. Insects or bits of buckskin were occasionally applied to a sore, and heat therapy was used in the form of hot stones. In the treatment of arthritis, small cones of chewed-up wood were burned upon the affected joint.

Hal Ogle, a pioneer of Klamath Falls, had the unique experience of being treated for snow blindness by a conjurer. His treatment, which was given at Klamath Marsh, is explained in full on a tape recording in the Klamath County Museum. In brief, the treatment consisted of steam therapy and a song which Ogle has reproduced almost as well as the conjurer who treated him . . . And, yes, he recovered his vision.

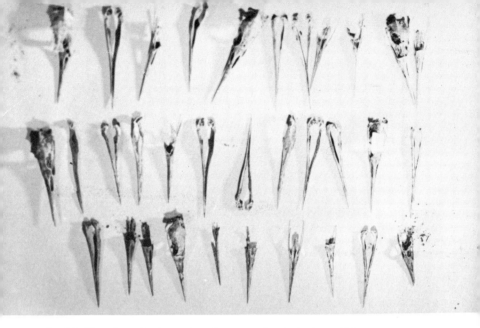

Fig. 168. These heron heads may have been part of a cloak of a medicine man.

Fig. 169. Large mammal-bone beads stained with red paint.

With today's patients, the shaman might provoke more mirth than awe, yet the numbers of cures must have been impressive. If the cure is real, the dress of the practitioner matters little, be it from wearers of heron heads or starched white jackets. The well-known conjurers were able to charge handsome fees for their services, but the liability for failure was considerably more severe than a mere malpractice suit. Property indemnity for a life might be demanded by relatives of the deceased, or even death might be the accepted penalty for failure. Charles Drew told of the killing of Doctor George, an Indian shaman, by Henry Jackson, a Klamath Indian. Jackson's claim, when he was tried for murder, was that the Indian doctor had caused his two daughters to die, and he was only rightfully seeking retribution.

Disposal of the Dead

Cremation places and burials testify to many unsuccessful medical treatments. Many Indians died in infancy and many more before they reached adulthood. The lament of the mourners must have been heard many times about the shores and on the islands of the lake.

The uncovering of burial places has revealed that, over the ages, the funeral practices of the Modocs have gone through four phases. The earliest form of the disposal of the dead was simple burial in individual graves at the village site. This was changed to the practice of cremation in house pits or on points around the lake. The third phase was to carry the dead to a high point near the village for the cremation ceremony. The last phase, that of burial with Christian services, resulted from the teaching of the missionaries. The Christian burial did not come about as an abrupt change. Charles Drew related that Indians often conducted their own tribal funeral service in addition to the Christian service. Harley Zeller, long-time Methodist minister at the Williamson River Mission, said that the vocal lamentations were an accepted part of a funeral even into the 1940s.

Prior to the adoption of the Christian burial service, the funeral and its attendant ceremonies were of greater social significance than they are today. The importance and wealth of the deceased had a great deal to do with the type of service, the number of mourners, and the amount of offerings. Many were buried with no offerings; these so-called "mother-in-law" burials could very possibly have been slaves or very old people.

For those with relatives, carefully arranged funerals were conducted by both Klamaths and Modocs. The pattern involved removal of the dead to the place of cremation and placing the remains on a carefully prepared fire. Those in attendance carried on mourning chants while placing the offerings on the funeral pyre, along with the goods of the deceased. The fragments of broken mortars, pestles, pipes, and knives indicate that much of the goods was purposely broken before placement on the grave. Some have said that the purpose of the breakage was to kill the object in order that it could accompany its owner after death. Others have felt that breakage was to guard against robbery of the grave—as broken objects would have had little value.

Some burials which preceded the cremation showed that a red paint was thrown over the corpse. The large, decorated mammal-bone beads from the Payne collection (Fig. 169) show the use of the red pigment.

Customs of the Mourners

Following a funeral, the principal mourners were required by tradition to visit a sweat bath for purification rites for five days. If a widow survived, she was to have pitch placed upon her hair to assure a proper period of mourning. After this interval, she was to marry the brother of the deceased. This marriage custom seems strange today, but the strict division of work between males and females in those times made marriage an urgent matter. Men were not to gather roots and wocas; women were not to hunt. The protective function of the male was of prime importance. This marriage custom also solved the problem of the orphan and the broken home; in fact, it seemed to be a social custom designed to help preserve the human species.

Confirming the fact that Indian services were occasionally very simple or entirely lacking, Peter Skene Ogden made some comments in his Journal, December 11, 1826—giving a report on the habits of the Klamaths, as well as some philosophy of his own: ". . . in my travels last year I observed the Snakes did not bury their dead and the same remark holds good with the Clammette Nation and what not only surprised me but what appeared most strange was to see within ten yards of one of their huts three skulls and within nearly as short a distance of another hut I saw two, nor did they appear of a very old date. This is as it ought to be—the living and dead remain together and act as a warning to them that sooner or later they must also die. Had we constantly the same remaining before us probably our sins would be less in number than they are now, but again it would soon fail of having any effect for we would soon come familiar and lay no stress on skulls."

Knowing the habits of the Klamaths, some have suggested that the skulls observed by Ogden were those of enemies which had been brought in as trophies to be used in dancing activities. The possibility also exists that they were the remains of incomplete house-pit cremations.

Wealth Often Buried or Burned

The Pueblo Indians of the Southwest deposited their dead under the floors of their houses, or in pockets of their cliff dwellings. Possibly for the same reasons the ancestors of the Modocs and Klamaths used the village sites for the deposit of their dead. The eroded islands of Lower Klamath Lake show extensive use by both the living and the dead. Here the duck bones and the fish bones of the kitchen midden often mingle with the former possessions and offerings for the dead. Frank Hibben, the scientist of Sandia Cave fame, in New Mexico, said that it is fortunate for archeologists that primitive men were careless housekeepers and were also often careless in the handling of their dead; otherwise many of their tools and utensils would not have been lost and thus made available for future study. Nowhere have Hibben's remarks been better verified than in the cutting winds of Lower Klamath Lake, for the cremation islands and living quarters there reveal an ancient trade pattern different from, and more extensive than, that found anywhere else in the Klamath Highland.

Modoc Money

The medium of exchange or "money" of the prehistoric Indian was, for the most part, in the form of seashell beads. Woodpecker scalps were also used as a standard of wealth, but the shells were so widely accepted that even the white traders used some in dealing with the Indians. As if some stone-age economist had listed the characteristics of good money, the worked shells and ornaments came surprisingly close to the requirements of "good money" in present-day exchange. Their seashell money was easily stored, had lasting quality, was easily transported, could not be counterfeited, and was readily accepted by other people and tribes by virtue of its attractiveness.

The most universally exchanged shell money was the dentalium shown in Fig. 170. The seashore animal responsible for these shells was caught by coastal tribes off the shore of Vancouver Island. The shells were called Allicochick by the Indians and were sometimes carved to add to their value; also, the longer the shell, the greater the value. Indian men occasionally had tattoo marks on the arm to be used as a standard for the length of the dentalium.

If the dentalium was the most valued, the most common shell bead was the olivella. This seashell could rapidly be converted to a bead by grinding the sharp end off with a stone. One burial was associated with a length of over fifty feet of olivella beads. The beads were usually carried in strings of matched sizes, individual beads ranging in size from one-fourth to one inch in

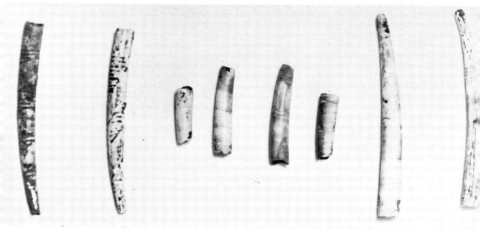

Fig. 170. Dentalium shells—the "standard money" of the West Coast Indians.
(Van Landrum photo)

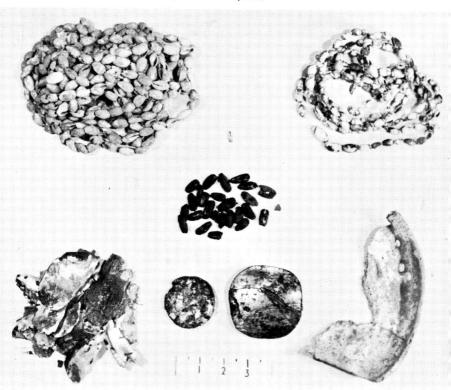

Fig. 171. Olivella, pine-nut, and abalone beads.

length. Fig. 171 shows a number of types of native wealth found on the Lower Klamath. At the upper left of the picture are unburned olivella shells before the cremation ceremony. At the upper right are olivella of a smaller type that have been burned. The dark beads in the center are pinon (pine) nut beads. Since this species of pine is not native to the Klamath area, they must have been traded from the slopes of the Sierra Nevada Range.

Raw abalone shells evidently had an exchange value similar to that which a raw, precious stone or metal might have today. Some have been found that are bored for stringing, whereas others were unworked in any way. At the lower left of Fig. 171 is unworked abalone shell. From the number of unworked pieces of this shell, it must be concluded that it had a bulk value. Some of the pieces were perforated for stringing and shaped like those in the lower center of the figure. The large, broken shell appears to have been a neck pendant or breast plate. The many shapes of cut abalone shell beads are illustrated in Fig. 172. Most have single perforations, but a few have two holes for stringing.

In addition to grinding off the end of the olivella shell and making it into simple beads, the stone-age jewelers used a more difficult method to get more beads from their material. They split each shell and made two beads as shown in Fig. 173, No. 5. The figure also illustrates an even harder process of utilizing these shells by cutting them into small round disks (Nos. 1, 2, 3, 4, and 6). The Modocs never seemed to have discovered any way to mass-produce these disks; each bead shows unmistakable signs of having been individually fashioned. None are perfectly round; none are perfectly perforated in the center.

The method of stringing both shell-shaped and disk beads was also utilized to "stretch" the material. Fig. 174, from the collection of Harvey Greenbank of Tule Lake, California, shows such beads which were frozen into their original arrangement by the cremation fire. The disks were evidently strung on two cords

Fig. 172. Abalone shell was cut into many designs.

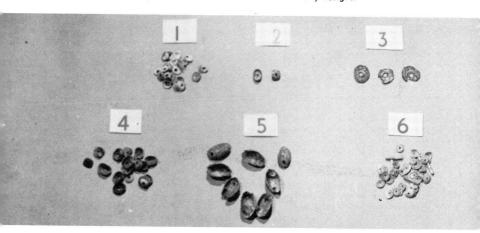

Fig. 173. Disc beads of varied shapes.

Fig. 174. (below) Novel methods of stringing are revealed in these beads, frozen by the ages.

in a manner that would cause them to be side by side, rather than flat against each surface.

Three species of shells are strung in the necklace in Fig. 175. Short pieces of dentalium are interspersed with small disk beads. The unusual-shaped crescents of abalone shell have been perforated in a vertical fashion so that they could be strung like a neckerchief slide. The eagle claws show no sign of perforation as the outer horny covering has been decayed away, leaving only the bony part of the claw. They may have been stitched to an article of clothing rather than worn as beads. The small clams (*glycymeris*) have all been drilled for stringing. This type of bead is relatively rare on Lower Klamath. The two perforated shells on either side of the crescents in the figure are thinner than most abalone shells and are believed to be a species of northern abalone.

Bone Ornaments

An unusual bead fashion is shown in the rectangular cut abalone in Fig. 176. Each bead is about one inch long. The curved horn object above the beads is perforated on each end; it is called an arm band by collectors. Some of these bands are quite broad as illustrated by the fragment at the right of the figure. The piece at the left is the broken end of another arm band. The hole for attachment is visible, but the ornamental carving hardly shows. Another group of these curved artifacts, from the Payne Collection, is shown in Fig. 177. These are much narrower and have been decorated. No positive use, other than ornamental, is known for these strange objects. The ends have holes drilled in them, apparently to serve as a point of attachment.

Beads made from bird and mammal bones were used by the island people before trade with tribes from the Pacific developed. Some of the bone beads were well formed, decorated, and highly polished from long use. Other bones were so poorly fashioned

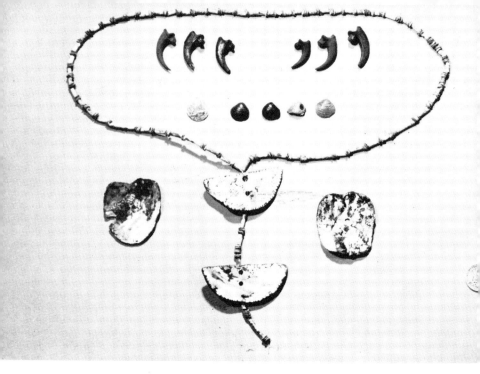

Fig. 175. Bird claws, drilled clam shells, and abalone pendants.

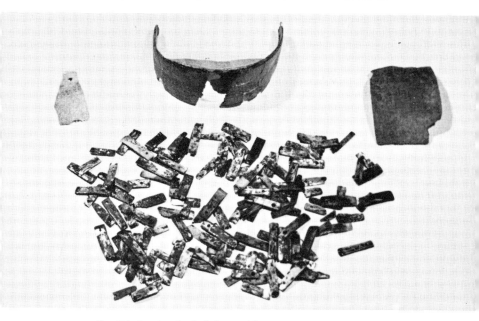

Fig. 176. Arm bands of elk horn, with some unusual rectangular beads.

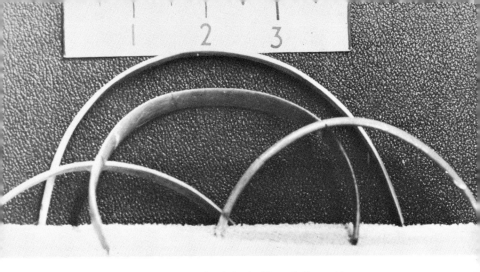

Fig. 177. Antler or bone arm bands in the Klamath County Museum.

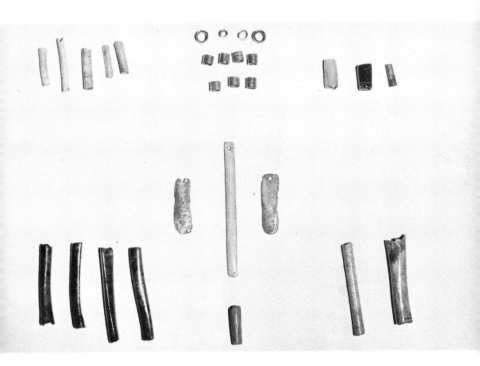

Fig. 178. Bone beads took many shapes.

into beads that they could hardly be distinguished as beads. Some idea of the variety can be seen in Fig. 178.

Bone decorations must have been interspersed with shell types, or used singly by the wearers, because complete sets of bone types are exceedingly rare. The long, polished flat-bone pendant in the center of Fig. 178 is called a head scratcher. These bones were suspended from a string about the neck and were used by the women of the tribe during times when they were forbidden by taboo from touching their hair. For example, touching the hair was taboo following the birth of a child. The shorter pendants in the figure were probably ornamental in purpose, as are those pictured in Fig. 179. It is, of course, impossible to distinguish between a head scratcher and some of the ornaments.

A most unusual set of mammal-bone beads is shown in Fig. 180; it is known as "The Fiddler's Green Necklace," and was discovered near Clear Lake by Ward Payne when he was only five years old. His father, Frank Payne, recovered the necklace from the soil in the same order in which the original wearer had strung the bones. It is now on display at the Klamath County Museum.

The lavaliere—shown in Fig. 181 and owned by Jim DeVore— is a rare red stone bead which has three points of attachment. DeVore found it on the south shore of the lake while hunting mushrooms. The circle-and-dot design is a familiar one, but the perforated point for the suspension of another string is unusual.

Nose Ornaments

Many Modocs and Klamaths had the septum of the nose pierced in order to introduce a dentalium shell to be worn in the nose. The lower objects in Fig. 182 are thought to be nose pieces. Two are of steatite, one of bone. The one above No. 3 is jade. They are part of the Clifford Clayton family collection, as are the decorated bone and stone pieces in the top part of the figure. No native jade is found in the Klamath Highland and such objects are quite rare. A few pendants of this material have been found in the Lower Klamath area. One of the most beautiful,

Fig. 179. Bone pendants were carved according to the fancy of the maker.
(Van Landrum photo)

Fig. 180. (below) "Fiddler's Green Necklace," of mammal bones. (From Payne Collection in Klamath County Museum)

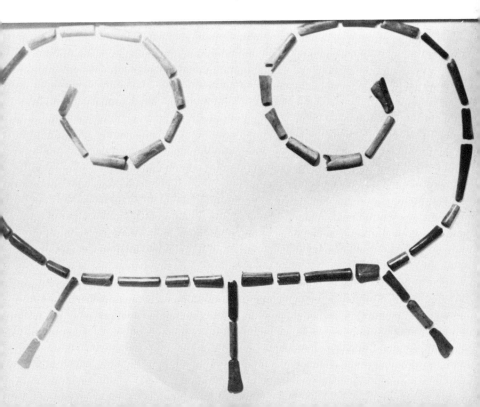

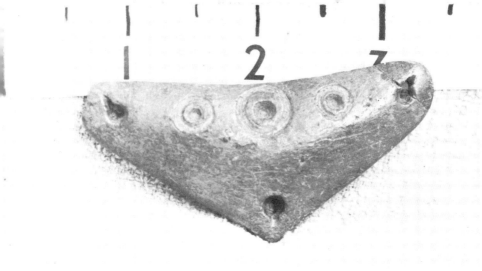

Fig. 181. Red stone bead of unique design from the Jim DeVore Collection.
(Van Landrum photo)

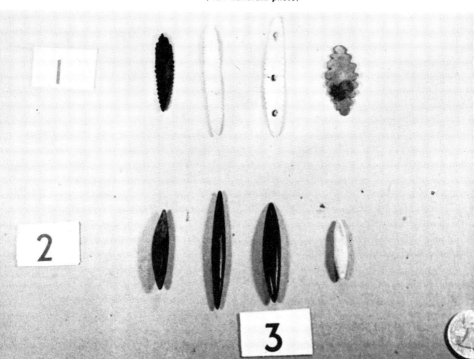

Fig. 182. Ornaments and nose pieces.

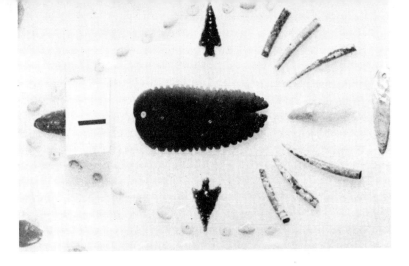

Fig. 183. Jade pendant carved in an unusual design.

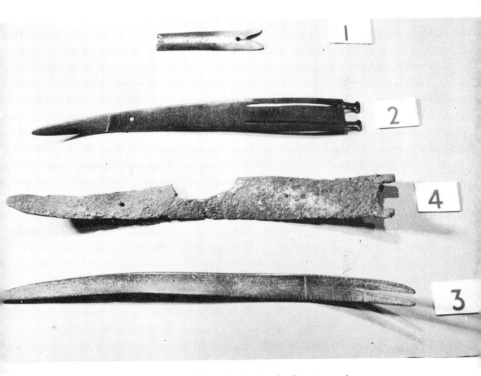

Fig. 184. Bone pieces believed to be shuttles for net weaving.

Fig. 183, was found by Sam Merriman of Merrill, Oregon. No one seems to know the origin of the jade material. The dentalia shells in the figure provide a scale for comparison.

Bone Tools

The salmon runs in the Klamath River never equaled those in the Columbia. Nevertheless, they were an important source of wealth and stability to those Indians whose villages enabled them to take the fish. Many methods, including the net, were used to catch the fish. The unusual bone tools in Fig. 184 are believed to be shuttles used in the manufacture of nets. A common feature of the shuttle is the pronged extension at the back for holding the cordage which was used in weaving the net. No. 1, the broken fragment, has a perforation near the divided end. No. 2, from the Gienger Collection, and No. 4, the property of Dick Meeker, have the perforation toward the pointed end. The bottom shuttle, No. 3, has no hole for string but has two distinct marks spaced two inches apart which are thought to be used as a measurement for the mesh of the nets.

The bone objects, Nos. 5-8 in Fig. 185, may also have been used in net making. They seem too large for ornaments or head scratchers. Dr. Claude Schaffer, former curator of the Klamath County Museum, suggested their use as a "bull roarer." This practice was in vogue among Midwest Indians who twirled a flat stone or stick about their heads with a string to make a roaring noise. Some of these large spatula-shaped bones are perforated for attachment. There seems to be no other evidence suggesting that the "bull roarer" was a part of Modoc tradition. Nos. 1-4 in this figure show another view of the shuttles appearing in Fig. 184.

The scarcity of bone needles throughout the Klamath Highland can be accounted for in some measure by the fact that tules, rather than leather or cloth, were the basic material for clothing. In Fig. 186, the eye has been burned from the second needle from the left. The small needle at the far right is from green

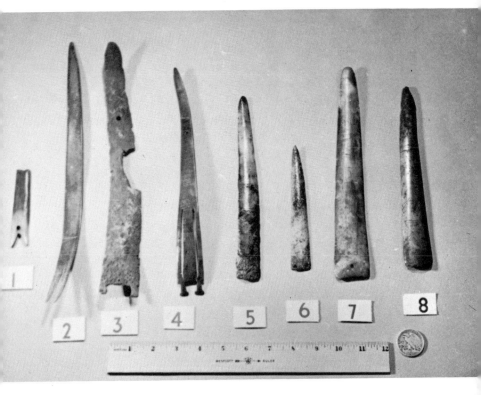

Fig. 185. Shuttles and long pendant-like objects.

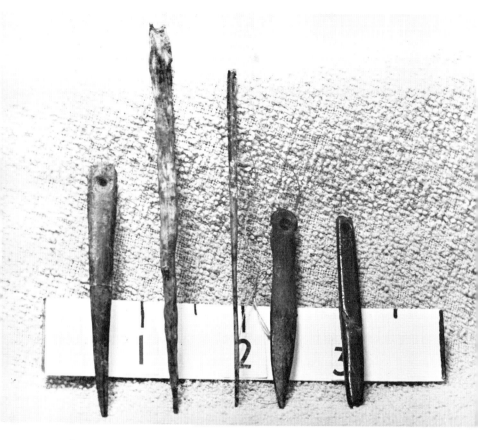

Fig. 186. Bone needles were much rarer than awls or punches. (Van Landrum photo)

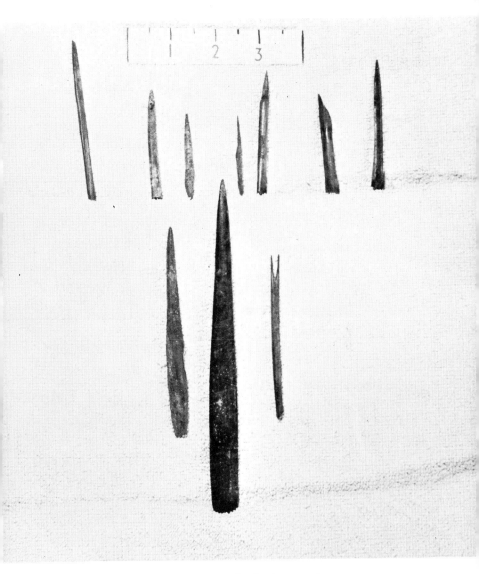

Fig. 187. Pickle fork with other bone punches.

fossilized bone from the bed of Silver Lake. The slender needle in the center has such a tiny eye that only the smallest of thread could be admitted. This, in itself, attests the quality of the nettle-fiber cordage. The needle at the far left of the figure and the second from the right are substantial enough to have been used as awls. Ordinarily the bone awls had no eye for threading, and were longer.

If needles were scarce, the opposite could be said of bone punches or perforators. Those in the top of Fig. 187 are made of bird bone. The large polished bone in the center at the bottom has been highly decorated as though to be used for an ornament or hairpin. The "pickle fork" on the lower right is the only one known to exist. The bone at the lower left has a slight bevel and could have been used as a projectile point. However, the point is sharper than that usually found on arrows so it is believed to be a basketry awl.

Bird-bone splinter awls are quite common, but a strange and prevalent custom was the insertion of one bird bone within another. Some had points ground upon them as though to be used as an awl; others were simply unworked bone. The practice of putting one bone inside another was perhaps related to such good-luck charm as our present-day wishbone or horseshoe.

Root Gathering

The gathering of roots was the work of woman. The principal roots used were: ipos, camas, and kol (pronounced coal)—a parsnip-shaped root said to be nutritious and also to protect the user from attacks by bears. Mrs. O. T. Anderson, Sr., of Beatty, told the writer that kol smelled worse than limburger cheese but tasted very good to those courageous enough to get close to it. The roots were removed from the ground by the use of a digging stick. Since some grew to considerable depth, more than average pressure on the stick was required. The antler objects in Fig. 188 were used for the top handles of the digging sticks. They enabled